Understanding and Managing the Therapeutic Relationship

Also available from Oxford University Press

PSYCHOEDUCATION IN MENTAL HEALTH
by Joseph Walsh

STRAIGHT TALK ABOUT PROFESSIONAL ETHICS
by Kim Strom-Gottfried

ENDINGS IN CLINICAL PRACTICE: EFFECTIVE CLOSURE IN
DIVERSE SETTINGS, 2/e
by Joseph Walsh, foreword by Thomas M. Meenaghan

SECONDARY TRAUMATIC STRESS AND THE
CHILD WELFARE PROFESSIONAL
by Josephine G. Pryce, Kimberly K. Shackelford, and David H. Pryce

WHAT IS PROFESSIONAL SOCIAL WORK?
by Malcolm Payne

EVIDENCE-BASED PRACTICES FOR SOCIAL WORKERS
by Thomas O'Hare

AN EXPERIENTIAL APPROACH TO GROUP WORK
by Rich Furman, Diana Rowan, and Kimberly Bender

SHORT-TERM EXISTENTIAL INTERVENTION IN CLINICAL PRACTICE
by Jim Lantz and Joseph Walsh

MINDFULNESS AND SOCIAL WORK
edited by Steven Hick

SOCIAL WORK PRACTICE IN NURSING HOMES
by Julie Sahlins

THERAPEUTIC GAMES AND GUIDED IMAGERY
by Monit Cheung

Understanding and Managing the Therapeutic Relationship

Fred McKenzie

Aurora University

OXFORD
UNIVERSITY PRESS

Oxford University Press is a department of the University of Oxford.
It furthers the University's objective of excellence in research, scholarship,
and education by publishing worldwide.

Oxford   New York
Auckland   Cape Town   Dar es Salaam   Hong Kong   Karachi
Kuala Lumpur   Madrid   Melbourne   Mexico City   Nairobi
New Delhi   Shanghai   Taipei   Toronto

With offices in
Argentina   Austria   Brazil   Chile   Czech Republic   France   Greece
Guatemala   Hungary   Italy   Japan   Poland   Portugal   Singapore
South Korea   Switzerland   Thailand   Turkey   Ukraine   Vietnam

Oxford is a registered trade mark of Oxford University Press
in the UK and certain other countries.

Published in the United States of America by
Oxford University Press
198 Madison Avenue, New York, NY 10016

© Oxford University Press 2016

The painting on the cover is a watercolor by Richard Hull.

Library of Congress Cataloging-in-Publication Data

McKenzie, Fred R.
    Understanding and managing the therapeutic relationship / Fred McKenzie ; foreword
by Chuck Zastrow.
        p. ; cm.
    Includes bibliographical references and index.
    ISBN 978-0-19-061607-6 (pbk. : alk. paper)
    1. Psychotherapist and patient. I. Title.
    [DNLM: 1. Psychotherapy. 2. Professional-Patient Relations. 3. Psychological
Theory. WM 420 M47845u 2011]
    RC480.8.M393 2011
    616.89'14—dc22
                                                                2010008633

To my wonderful wife, Tamela, for her enduring love,
patience, and support

Contents

Foreword

UNDERSTANDING AND MANAGING THE
THERAPEUTIC RELATIONSHIP

What causes positive changes in counseling and psychotherapy? This may be the most important question confronting counselors/psychotherapists! As yet, there is no definitive answer. However, there is considerable research evidence suggesting that it is not the particular therapy approaches that are being used, but instead it is the nature of the relationship between the client and the counselor (Hubble, Duncan, & Miller, 2009). If this research is accurate, then it is essential that clinical practitioners focus greater attention on developing the kind of relationship with clients that will best facilitate clients making positive changes in their lives.

Many texts and professional articles have been written on therapeutic relationships. Why the need for an additional text? Dr. Fred McKenzie's text, *Understanding and Managing the Therapeutic Relationship*, is the first text that takes a comprehensive look at the vast array of the theories and components of a therapeutic relationship. This text covers the following theories and components: attachment theory, object relations theory, self-psychology, Rogerian therapy and theory, neuroscience theory, the relational template, engagement and attachment, the treatment plan, transference, countertransference, self-disclosure, cultural competence, diversity, closure and termination, transitions, managing losses, using the *Diagnostic and Statistical Manual* (American Psychiatric Association, 2000), and using the *Psychodynamic Diagnostic Manual* (Alliance of Psychoanalytic Organizations, 2006).

This text should be required reading for all clinical practitioners and for students enrolled in programs to become clinical practitioners. It is an encyclopedia of the theories and components of therapeutic relationships. In addition, McKenzie presents several case examples that illustrate the theories and components. In a nutshell, if a clinical practitioner (or a student studying to be a clinical practitioner) wants to further develop his or her therapeutic relationship skills, this is the text to read!

Every clinical practitioner has an ethical obligation to seek to facilitate positive changes in clients. This text provides considerable material on how to facilitate such positive changes.

Charles Zastrow, PhD, LCSW
Professor of Social Work and Assistant Director of the
MSW Program at George Williams College of Aurora University

Preface

There have been many texts written about the initial stages of the therapeutic relationship (*Direct Social Work Practice* [Hepworth, Rooney, & Larsen, 2006], *The Skills of Helping Individuals, Families, Groups and Communities* [Shulman, 2009], and *The Practice of Social Work* [Zastrow, 1999]). All of them are excellent in their own right, describing the theoretical approaches to engaging the client in counseling or therapy and/or the specific techniques and skills necessary to establishing a successful working alliance in various forms of treatment. The theories are valuable and explanatory, and the techniques are oftentimes empirically researched and even validated to a sufficient extent. However, something is missing.

Most of these well-written and well-intentioned texts do not sufficiently address the emotional elements of the therapeutic relationship that function as the glue that holds it together. Furthermore, there is little, if any, attention paid to explaining the purpose of the emotional element in the therapeutic relationship, its origins in attachment, the human brain, and the ongoing necessity for it throughout life. This book fills that important gap.

Understanding and Managing the Therapeutic Relationship is a primer. This text is designed to complement many of the other quality textbooks intended to orient the beginning practitioner to clinical practice. When used in conjunction with some of the other texts mentioned earlier and others, *Understanding and Managing the Therapeutic Relationship* provides a comprehensive approach to help the beginning clinician thoroughly understand and implement the theories and techniques so essential to effective practice with clients of all ages and backgrounds.

Key to the process of understanding the rationale for clinical practice is deciphering the complicated emotions that all practitioners experience in their relationships with clients, regardless of how long they have been practicing. In fact, understanding those subtle and intense emotional reactions is the key to any successful therapeutic endeavor. The ability of any therapist to perceive, understand, and appropriately react to the client's emotions can make the difference between success and failure in counseling from the very first session.

This text addresses theory and technique in clinical work but also something more. This text goes to great lengths to explain the intricacies of the emotional elements inherent in the therapeutic exchange between the therapist and client and, more important, to illustrate the origins of those processes.

Attachment, neuroscience, and key psychodynamic theories are essential to understanding the biological predispositions for emotional engagement in all human beings. Everyone is prewired to a greater or lesser extent from birth to emotionally connect with others. That ability is essential for survival in a social world. Breakdowns in signaling, empathy, recognition, and other overt and subtle forms of communication form the basis of most human difficulties. Therapy helps modify, correct, and/or repair those problems so that one can be more adaptive and effective in their respective worlds.

The effectively trained therapist should be knowledgeable about not only the theories and techniques of counseling and psychotherapy but also about the crucial underpinnings that form the core of those theories; namely attachment, neuroscience, and key psychodynamic theories. Only a thorough understanding of those key theories can equip the clinician with the knowledge necessary to make sense of the complex emotions that occur within and between the therapist and the client.

This text addresses at length those emotional exchanges and their multifaceted meanings as they relate to the development of the initial therapeutic relationship.

Acknowledgments

Much of this book is the result of many years of thoughtful clinical practice and study throughout my career. Since the very beginnings of my professional life, I have intuitively understood the value and importance of the therapeutic relationship as a key curative factor in practice. My dissertation finally gave me the opportunity to study that notion in some small way. This text is a much stronger yield of the fruit of that process.

I want to thank Jerry Lipsch, my first mentor, for helping me understand the power of the therapy relationship. Dr. Al Lang, my first consulting psychiatrist, was invaluable in allowing me to really experience the process of the clinical encounter. Lynn Barron was my therapist for many years. I would not be the person I am today without her unconditional empathic attunement.

Dr. Randy Lucente, Dr. Joe Walsh, and Dr. Sally Bonkowski were the members of my dissertation committee at Loyola University in Chicago. I want to especially thank Randy for his patient guidance beginning in my MSW program at George Williams College in Downers Grove, Illinois, and eventually at Loyola. I am deeply indebted to him.

Of course, I owe so much to the numerous clients who taught me so much over my three decades of clinical experience.

Finally, I want to thank my wife, Tamela, for her second editing (she also was the first reader on my adolescent book). Her unconditional love and support is what moves my life.

The Theoretical and Empirical Underpinnings of the Therapeutic Relationship

Barb walks into the counseling room appearing shy and awkward to the therapist. He had somewhat expected this, given the brief phone call in which they had both discussed Barb's initial concerns and reasons for seeking therapy. Barb, in her late twenties, had informed the therapist that she suffered from severe anxiety and that she wanted to see a professional who could help her manage those emotions and deal effectively with them in her life, as well. The therapist had assured her that he was experienced with this sort of difficulty and that he would certainly do his best to help Barb. Barb did not seem reassured on the phone but agreed to come to a therapy appointment.

Barb sat down on the couch, and in a nonverbal way, she suggested that she was extremely tentative and uneasy about being there. For example, she sat on the edge of the couch, shaking her legs, and she had an expression on her face that seemed frightened. It felt to the therapist as if she might bolt from the room at any minute. In other words, the emotional state of the client seemed to the therapist to indicate extreme anxiety.

Sensing Barb's extreme anxiety, the therapist decided to say something to help put her at ease. "Tell me a little bit about what brings you here," he said.

"You know," said Barb. "We talked about it over the phone, remember?" This felt rather defensive, and the therapist was not quite sure how to respond to such a disarming remark.

"Well," said the therapist, "I do remember you saying something about wanting to work on anxiety issues and also wanting to make sure that I knew something about that condition. Would you like to tell me a bit more about some of the circumstances that have contributed to this problem?"

"No," said Barb. "I don't think I feel ready to do that just yet."

The therapist felt entirely disarmed. "What am I supposed to say now?" he thought. He knew it was his role to try and engage the client, but this client didn't seem to want to engage, yet she didn't seem to want to leave either. What now?

"OK," said the therapist. "What would you like to talk about then?"

"I don't know," said Barb. "You're the therapist."

"That's right Barb, but I can't possibly know what you may want to talk about," said the therapist. "I also feel at a bit of a loss if you can't tell me what's on your mind."

"Yeah, that's a problem isn't it?" said Barb. "Well, maybe after I get to know you better I'll feel comfortable opening up to you—maybe not, too."

"This is really frustrating and challenging," thought the therapist. He had seen hundreds of clients over the years, and he sensed that this one was going to be especially challenging. He intuitively understood that she was resistant in the most traditional manner, but that was such a simplistic way to describe Barb. Doing so reduced her to a stereotype rather than helping provide a humanistic understanding of her plight.

The therapist thought that Barb was probably afraid, anxious, and angry, as well as needy and dependent. She truly seemed to want to be there, but she was not available to communicate any emotions directly, as her evasive, sarcastic, and off-putting comments evidenced. However, the subtleness of her speech mannerisms signaled the therapist that Barb wanted to be there. For instance, she challenged the therapist on his ability to help her, but when he questioned her directly about her need for treatment, she acknowledged that she wanted help.

The therapist recognized the subtlety of the client's communications from more than thirty years of clinical work with many types of clients who communicate in cryptic and protective interactive styles. The key to engaging such clients is to be patient, to not push the interactions, and to wait for a therapeutic relationship to develop over time.

"OK, Barb," said the therapist. "Let's take it slow."

"What does that mean?" asked Barb.

"I think it means that we talk about things you want to talk about, when you feel ready," said the therapist.

"Isn't that going to be a waste of my time?" wondered Barb.

"Well, maybe," said the therapist, "but I don't know of any other way to proceed if you don't feel ready or comfortable with therapy yet."

"Good point," said Barb. "However, I've got some questions I want to ask you about how you do therapy, or more exactly, what you believe in. Is that cool to talk about in here?"

"I guess so," said the therapist.

So began the therapeutic relationship with Barb several years ago. She was a very trying client, to say the least. I felt compelled to help her. I knew instinctively I could help her given my experience and the similar clients whom I had worked with over the years. I knew the work was going to be difficult, tedious, time consuming, frustrating, and quite possibly very helpful and rewarding.

Had this been a case early on in my professional career, I would have been terrified, felt horribly incompetent, and probably tried to find every way possible to remove myself from the situation. I believe that is the response of all new counselors with similar cases. Before the clinician has developed a comprehensive repertoire of knowledge, skill, and experience, he or she cannot possibly be an effective clinician with clients such as Barb, or with any others.

Barb's situation brings to mind many of the crucial theories, techniques, and empirical information necessary to understand and effectively help such clients lead a happier life. This chapter examines the key paradigms and knowledge bases that are so essential to helping beginning clinicians engage, manage, and understand their important role in the therapeutic process.

ATTACHMENT THEORY

The studies on attachment by Bowlby (1969) and Ainsworth, Blehar, Waters, and Wall (1978) were instrumental in identifying and recognizing the necessity of the primary attachment relationship. Through careful study and research, attachment theorists have been able to demonstrate that all human beings need a strong emotional bond with primary caretakers to establish a healthy emotional self. Through the attachment process of development in infancy, human beings learn how to manage their emotional selves. Attachment theorists have been able to identify four key types of attachment styles, whether constitutional or developmentally based, that are present in early development.

In an emotionally healthy environment, caretakers physically and emotionally respond to infants in such a way that infants experience the world as a relatively safe place. Healthy caretakers are cued into infants' physical and emotional messages. The ensuing dance that occurs between primary caretakers and infants sets the stage for a sense of emotional safety and consistency in the infant's world (Fosha, Siegal, & Solomon, 2009).

Secure attachment describes those infants who are comfortable relating to others, especially primary caretakers. They are not anxious, uncomfortable, or avoidant in their behaviors with people. Instead, these infants enjoy and thrive on interactions with others because they have been able to establish the type of relationship mentioned earlier. Secure attachment is considered the most normal attachment state in early development.

Infants who are anxious in their attachment tend to behave in ways that signal strong discomfort in their interactions, and they are not easily soothed by their caretakers. Such infants tend to feel anxiety, or even threatened, in interactions with key caretakers. This behavior can oftentimes be improved through an attuned relationship with a caretaker who is able to empathically respond to and soothe the infant through voice, touch, and a general secure atmosphere of interaction.

Behaviors intended to distance oneself from another person characterize avoidant attachment. Infants with this type of attachment style do not appear interested in emotionally connecting with others; in fact, they seem disinterested in most human interactions. This type of behavior is often associated with anxiety, as well.

Infants that display disorganized attachment appear chaotic, erratic, and odd in their ability and interest in human interaction. Their behavior can seem illogical and without purpose. Such infants appear to have the most troubled interactive style.

Attachment styles can be constitutional, or developmentally induced, as mentioned previously. The specific etiology of attachment styles is not clear. All infants are born with a certain attachment predisposition. In fact, it is much more accurate to describe attachment along a continuum from secure to disorganized. There are probably never distinctively absolute states but, instead, styles that are somewhere along the attachment continuum.

What is interesting, troubling, and challenging is that one can never know for certain from what or how the attachment configuration of early infancy derives. For example, an infant with constitutionally secure attachment could reasonably become anxious or avoidant through unresponsive caretaking, a deprived environment, or abuse and neglect. An infant with an anxious or avoidant attachment style might be able to develop a more securely attached style given attuned caretaking and a secure environment. The possibilities along this attachment continuum are quite disparate and extremely difficult to categorize in any concrete manner because of the complexities of environment, caretaker, and infant constitution. Recognizing and understanding the complex continuum of attachment and caretaking configurations becomes one of the great challenges for all therapists.

What does this discussion have to do with Barb? From a purely attachment theory standpoint, Barb can be characterized in several ways along the continuum. Attachment theory can help give the clinician one diagnostic lens with which to assess Barb by examining the therapeutic interaction in this first session. The therapist can merely examine his or her own emotional responses and interactions with Barb to begin to do this. Although one can't be sure, Barb does not appear to have a profoundly secure attachment style. She appears anxious; seems resistant or defensive in her interactions with the therapist; and is not willing, at least initially, to share much about herself, her feelings, and so on. I believe it is quite safe to say that Barb is not securely attached, at least in therapy.

Does Barb appear disorganized? Well, she might, except that she does say she wants to be in therapy and is interested in getting help. If she were nearer to the disorganized style, Barb's communication might not be easy to follow, she might not be able to articulate a clear plan, and her emotions might fluctuate a great deal. This does not seem to be the case with Barb. She may not be engaged, but she seems to demonstrate some type of goal-driven communication, albeit guarded and withholding.

Barb may best be described as anxious and avoidant. She seems to demonstrate the qualities of anxiety and avoidance in her interactions with the therapist. She is not simply anxious. She is not simply avoidant. Barb appears in this first session to have both elements in her interactive style.

Is this a definitive diagnostic profile? No, of course not. Is it useful information for a first therapy session? Yes. By pursuing a hypothesis based on attachment theory styles, the therapist might find that Barb is exhibiting some type of anxious-avoidant interactive style. The therapist can then decide to intervene in ways that will help Barb feel more secure and comfortable in opening up and engaging in therapy. This therapist attempted to do just that: I empathically responded to Barb's anxious-avoidant style by acknowledging her feelings and concerns, and by giving her the space she needed to feel comfortable enough to eventually engage in therapy.

Had I ignored Barb's anxious-avoidant manner, she may never have been able to establish a trusting bond for future work. A more carefully attuned and empathic approach to an anxious-avoidant attachment style may take time, but it will undoubtedly be more successful in the long run than insisting that the client respond to the traditional questions of the first session and interventions aimed at identifying the presenting concern, establishing discrete goals, and mapping future work. In other words, therapists need to continue to base their therapeutic responses and interactions to clients like Barb in a manner that validates and attempts to soothe and reassure them.

One might even venture to say that the therapist's attuned style is what the therapy should be about. After all, Barb did say over the phone that she had a problem with anxiety. Perhaps establishing an attuned and empathic relationship with Barb would help her manage her anxiety in ways that will eventually help her feel less anxious.

Attachment theory is but one of several key theories and approaches that can be useful in understanding the client's behavior in a first session. It can be a powerful diagnostic tool in directing the future course of treatment. Attachment theory is not the only paradigm to use with clients, but it can be an essential one.

OBJECT RELATIONS THEORY

Another valuable theoretical approach in working with Barb is object relations theory. Object relations theories have been around since the mid-twentieth century. They evolved out of psychoanalytic and ego psychology theory. The basic premise of object relations theory is very much in line with attachment theory. Object relations theorists believe that the emotional self of a human being develops through the internalization of relational aspects with primary caretakers. In other words, people learn how to soothe themselves and function in contextual autonomy by internalizing soothing, repetitive emotional interactions with key caretaking figures. Over time, this internalization develops into a relatively autonomous ability to self-soothe. The extent to which this internalization is successful in infancy and early childhood dictates the ability of an adult to function autonomously and to manage the wide range of complex human emotions (Greenspan & Shanker, 2006).

Although much of object relations theory was developed in the 1950s, recent empirical research and information have validated many of its major premises. In particular, neuroscience and attachment studies have indicated how attuned early relationships help establish the ability for emotionally healthy functioning (Alliance of Psychoanalytic Organizations, 2006). Several key object relations concepts are critical in helping understand the therapeutic relationship.

The infant develops object constancy through the repetitive internalizations of key aspects of the primary relationship with caretakers. Object constancy is a multifaceted concept. When infants attain this relative ability during the first few years of life, they are able to feel contextually secure when alone, and they are able to soothe themselves in the absence of primary caretakers (Mahler, Pine, & Bergman, 1975). This important ability is possible because infants have been able to establish mental representations of others that serve a self-soothing function. Only when infants have been able to form these kinds of early relationships can they function in a relatively emotionally secure fashion. The therapeutic relationship can be an obvious source of comfort and curative reparation for those clients who have suffered relational deficits, neglect, or abuse early in life.

Self constancy is another emotional ability that develops in this way. Through consistent, reliable, and positive interactions with key figures in life, infants are able to internalize a mental and emotional representation of self that is healthy and consistent. When they confront stress, disappointment, or other challenges in life, young children with self-constancy are able to retrieve positive and soothing images of self that help them weather difficult times. Children who have not been able to establish object or self-constancy struggle through life in continual anxiety, doubt, and even despair. The therapeutic relationship can help repair these problems by providing a secure, consistent, reliable, and positive holding environment (Winnicott, 1953). The holding environment is both a definition and a metaphor for the creation of a physically and emotionally secure and consistent world in which infants learn to feel safe and autonomous over time.

Sigmund Freud (1966) originated the theory of transference, or the ways patients distort the relationship with therapists on the basis of early memories and representations of primary caretakers. This form of resistance hinders patients from being able to uncover and work through deep-seated emotional conflicts until, with carefully timed interpretations of the analyst, they can unveil and understand them. Therapists' own emotional distortions, or countertransference, can also hinder therapists. For therapists, Freud thought, insight into their own emotional conflicts could help them be more available to clients in the therapeutic process. In other words, countertransference can be a good and useful tool if therapists handle it appropriately.

Heinrich Racker (1968) is well known for his comprehensive work on countertransference. He wrote extensively on the nature of countertransference and specific clinical techniques that could help clinicians use their own emotional reactions in the therapeutic process. Racker's work will be examined at greater length in subsequent chapters. Of particular importance, however, is his understanding of the nature of the psychological defense of projective identification.

Object relations theorists recognize that many clients project their thoughts, ideas, and emotions onto the therapist to protect themselves from intensely anxious elements. Therapists experience projective identification, a defensive reaction, through the relationship with the client both verbally and nonverbally. Body posture, tone of voice, and vitality affects (the quality of body movement) can unconsciously influence the therapist. This entire gestalt of interactions has the potential to create a certain tone or reaction to the client that can hinder the entire therapeutic process (Ogden, 1982; Stern, 1985; Tansey & Burke, 1989). Only through understanding the conscious and unconscious meanings of this communication can the therapist be helpful to the client.

Barb's behavior in the first session might be a form of projective identification. Her verbal and nonverbal communication certainly seem to be affecting the therapist and possibly interfering in the establishment of an attuned clinical relationship. It is far too early to tell whether these interactions can be understood as elements of projective identification, but silently holding on to those assumptions (based on thoughts and feelings experienced through interacting with the client) could be another helpful part of an initial assessment with this client. Object relations theory is another useful lens in viewing and understanding the clinical interaction.

RELATIONAL THEORY

Relational theory emphasizes the interactional matrix within the therapeutic relationship (Mitchell, 1988). The interactional matrix is the complex interplay of thoughts and emotions that are generated between client and therapist in the therapeutic encounter. Although not considered an exclusive object relations theory per se, relational work contains many of the same elements of that theory. Countertransference theory has evolved from the classical (therapists must identify and eliminate their own issues) to the totalist (countertransference is ubiquitous and must be recognized as a part of the treatment) to the contemporary notion that the intrapsychic and interpersonal relational aspects of therapist and client contribute to the therapeutic experience. Relational theory is a logical elaboration of this evolution.

It makes perfect intuitive sense that aspects of both the client and the therapist form the core of the clinical relationship. These elements are inseparable. When working with a client, the therapist must be keenly aware of the client, him- or herself, and the unique ways a real relationship is being created between the two of them. This complex matrix is an invaluable lens through which to formulate any assessment and intervention plan (Mitchell, 1988). The implication of these object relations concepts for clinical work will be discussed in much greater detail in subsequent chapters, which deal with engagement, the middle phase of treatment, and termination.

SELF-PSYCHOLOGY

Another psychological theory that is useful in understanding the therapeutic interaction is self-psychology. Heinz Kohut developed self-psychology in the 1970s. Kohut was practicing psychoanalysis with clients with narcissism at the University of Chicago when he discovered the new practice and developmental theory. While trying to use psychoanalytic techniques such as free association and withholding his interpretations in a timely fashion, Kohut found that this particular client group became increasingly more frustrated and even developed more severe problems. This impasse forced him to reformulate his clinical ideas, which eventually led him to develop the theory of self-psychology (Kohut, 1971).

Self-psychology is another clinical theory that focuses on emotional development. Kohut believed that all human beings are predisposed to internalize what he called self-objects throughout the life cycle, especially in childhood. Self-objects are the emotional representations derived from human interactions that become internalized into the self. The initial nuclear self (primitive original elements of self) develops from infancy into a cohesive self (a structure of self that is fundamentally able to self-soothe) through the internalization of self-objects. Humans needed self-objects, Kohut thought, just as they needed food and oxygen. In other words, infants could not develop in an emotionally healthy manner without them. As children grew up and were able to incorporate enough (quality and quantity) self-objects in their primary relationships with others, they needed those objects less. However, an ongoing need for self-objects in general continues throughout life. For example, an adult does not have the same ongoing need for validation as a child, but that need is always there in some form throughout life.

Kohut theorized that there were three types of self-objects. Mirroring self-objects come from validation one receives in primary relationships. For example, praising a young child who has successfully taken his or her first steps might be one form of self-object. Taken together over time, these positive self-object interactions can create a healthy sense of self in the child. Idealizing or merging self-objects represent the need to look up to, aspire to, and model oneself after another person. Usually these are primary caretakers, but they can be from any significant relationship in life. By emotionally merging with key figures, infants begin to internalize interactional elements that eventually become the self. For example, I can remember how special and important I felt just being with my grandmother. We didn't have to say a word. Just being close to her felt good, special, and soothing.

Twinship is the third self-object, one's need to have similar others in one's life. This sameness is a form of comfort and security that helps children, adolescents, and adults feel less alone and isolated. Knowing that others may share similar ideas, feelings, and experiences can be a powerful force in the development of identity. In the case of Barb, she may have felt less isolated if I would have shared that I, too, had felt uneasy, insecure, or suspicious in my own therapy.

A unique aspect of Kohut's theory is the notion that self-objects are essential throughout life. Although they are needed more in early development, self-objects become less necessary as one becomes able to incorporate enough of them. They are then able to draw from their own cohesive self to some extent to meet those self-object needs. This ability develops through a process that Kohut termed *transmuting internalization*. The rather daunting term means that, by internalizing sufficient self-objects in life and the subsequent optimal frustration that occurs in the human experience, one learns to trust and rely on one's own abilities, for the most part. Humans are never fully self-sufficient in terms of their self-object needs, but adequate transmuting internalization experiences enable them to live a relatively healthy emotional life (Kohut, 1971). Optimal frustration is the process by which children are able to draw on their own self-object reserves in the optimally timed absence of caretakers in times of stress. Singing a favorite song learned from a caring parent to comfort oneself in times of brief aloneness is an example of optimal frustration.

ROGERIAN THERAPY AND THEORY

A review of the models, theories, and paradigms most useful in helping the clinician understand and manage the therapeutic relationship would not be complete without Carl Rogers (1957), a psychologist who studied the role of empathy as a necessary and sufficient condition for healing in counseling. Rogers (1965) was instrumental in identifying, researching, and disseminating crucial information on the importance of empathy as a curative factor and technique in the therapy relationship. He pioneered clinical research that demonstrated the curative elements of using an empathic approach with the client. *Client-Centered Therapy*, originally published in 1951, was a groundbreaking book. The principles and techniques that Rogers researched and set forth in that text are still used today as part of training in most psychology and social work professional programs.

Rogers believed, and demonstrated, that active listening, reflective questioning, and empathic responses enabled clients to feel accepted enough to begin to trust and explore their own thoughts, feelings, and emotions in the relationship with their counselor. The nonjudgmental role of the counselor was essential to help clients trust and begin the process of self-exploration. In the example of Barb, she obviously needs this type of response from her therapist, if she will be able to trust enough to begin to even talk a little about what brings her to treatment. The counselor using Rogerian technique would seek to experience a vicarious empathic identification with Barb to be able to develop a trusting relationship. Only trust, security, and empathy will help such clients heal (Rogers, 1961).

The therapist's ability to recognize Barb's mixed feelings of anxiety and need, and to communicate with her in a way that demonstrates those needs, is an example of vicarious empathic identification. Most clinicians' ability to perform this type of intervention is a result of their own emotional and psychological awareness of self, especially as it relates to emotional reactions in life.

Eugene Gendlin was one of Rogers's disciples. He continued and expanded on Rogers's work, emphasizing the value of focusing on one's inner emotions as a guide to understanding the self and the client. Meditative in its principles and technique, focusing is an informative process for working in the therapeutic relationship by contemplating the therapist's thoughts and emotions in the present and how they may interface or inform an understanding with the client (Gendlin, 1978).

NEUROSCIENCE THEORY

Neuroscience is the study of the human brain. Recent advances in neuroscience theory and research have important implications for clinical practice, but the advances are particularly useful in helping clinicians understand and manage the therapeutic relationship. Freud implicitly understood that the models of the mind about which he theorized—specifically, id, ego, and superego—had physical locations in the actual human brain. Neuroscience was not advanced enough to confirm his notions at that time, but there is empirical evidence today to demonstrate that Freud's concepts have anatomical equivalents in the human brain (Cozolino, 2002).

For example, the amygdala, which is located in the limbic system between the brain stem and the cerebral cortex, serves many of the same functions that Freud might have designated to the id. Neuroscience theory and research has demonstrated that the human brain stem has evolved from the reptilian brain. It contains impulses and instincts that are based on primitive fight-or-flight responses. These impulses can be reinforced dramatically through repeated experiences of trauma, stress, and anxiety. As a result, humans who have suffered such experiences will have difficulty throughout life in handling relationships and/or situations that may trigger amygdala responses. Freud no doubt would have argued that this neurological function was the physical equivalent of the unconscious functioning of the id (Cozolino, 2002, 2006).

Ego functions might have been compared to some of the executive functions of the cerebral cortex, albeit the limbic system might have modulated many of them. The limbic system serves as a modifier of the emotions and impulses, filtering many of them before reaching the higher executive functions.

Laterality is another useful neuroscience concept. Human beings have a right and a left brain, which generally serve different functions. The right brain houses more of the feelings and creative aspects of the mind, whereas the left brain tends to be associated with more logical cognitive functioning. The corpus callosum connects the two halves of the brain and allows adequate communication between right and left brain (Cozolino, 2002, 2006).

Brain functioning is a complex matter that cannot be reduced to a simple summary. However, there tends to be a top-down and right-to-left process in the brain. In other words, behavior, feelings, thoughts, and emotions are communicated and managed through the right and left brain, as well as elements from the brain stem, amygdala and limbic system, and cerebral cortex. Most clinicians need to understand this sophisticated system to better manage the therapeutic relationship (Cozolino, 2002, 2006).

The client Barb might be acting more from her right brain, and the brain stem and amygdala, in demonstrating her cautiousness about sharing her story. A clinician who is fairly well versed in neuroscience would implicitly understand that a more aggressive or confrontational approach to engaging Barb would only reinforce that primitive response (stress). Instead, the therapist might try a gentler, slow-paced, empathic style to begin to modify Barb's reactions to treatment.

Several other key concepts from neuroscience are extremely relevant to understanding and managing the emotional aspects of the therapeutic relationship. Neural networks form from infancy well into adulthood, incorporating behavioral, emotional, and cognitive elements from life. As experiences become more repetitive, they inform anticipatory reactions in the mind. This form of intuition shapes how infants, children, adolescents, and adults handle their relationships with others.

The human infant's mind grows tens of thousands of neurons from the moment of birth and well into the late twenties. In fact, recent knowledge has pointed to neurogenesis, or the ability of neurons to develop throughout adulthood. The implication of this finding is that human beings can develop new neural networks throughout life. Thus, the psychotherapeutic relationship holds great promise for replacing existing neural networks that have been damaged or are in other ways deficient or maladaptive.

Neural plasticity explains the ability of the human brain to reroute or modify existing neural networks to repair problematic behavior, cognition, and/or emotion. In fact, looking at psychotherapy through the neuroscientific lens greatly enhances the entire realm. Clients can begin to modify their existing relational neural networks from the very moment of engagement with the therapist by experiencing new and healthier emotional experiences. Over time, those experiences begin to solidify into cognitive, emotional, and behavioral neural networks that reroute how clients experience the world and their relationships within it (Cozolino, 2002, 2006).

IMPLICATIONS FOR PRACTICE: THE RELATIONAL TEMPLATE

Taken together, the theories discussed here form a valuable template for understanding and performing competent clinical practice. The use of all the theories, models, and paradigms mentioned will enable therapists to begin to form a comprehensive picture of clients' inner emotional life. This process can help the clinician better assess clients and engage them in a helpful therapeutic process.

For example, working with Barb might seem less daunting if the therapist approaches the work from the perspective of the relational template. Through thoughtful examination of the components of the relational template, the clinician can formulate and intervene in a helpful therapeutic relationship. The clinician can approach Barb's hesitancy, anxiety, opposition, and avoidance in treatment with carefully timed verbal interventions aimed to provide a soothing, empathic contextual response.

Because Barb's presentation is particularly focused on her suspiciousness of treatment, the therapist should initially gear interventions toward helping her feel reassured about the therapeutic process and nothing more. Any initial move beyond is probably doomed to fail. However, once she begins to express some sense of trust and relief, the clinician can begin to explore some of the more traditional expectations of initial treatment, such as presenting concerns, background, goals of treatment, and so on. Of course, not every client is as challenging as Barb, but the relational template is an invaluable part of the repertoire for working with any type of clinical situation or practice model, be it cognitive behavioral therapy, family therapy, or psychodynamic therapy.

The informed clinician can begin to experiment with a variety of interventions drawn from the theories and models discussed in this chapter. Self-psychology interventions aimed at responding to self-object deficits or hunger can take the form of mirroring, merging or idealizing, and/or twinship responses. For example, Barb may initially need a preponderance of mirroring interventions to help validate her anxiety. Rogerian empathic techniques satisfy this need as well. The therapist's response—"OK, Barb, let's take it slow"—is a perfect example of a mirroring or empathic response aimed to reassure clients in their need to feel safe. A better response would have been, "You seem quite concerned about whether this is a safe place to open up." Carefully timed empathic interventions better address the client's need to feel safe and secure.

From a neuroscience standpoint, empathic responses soothe anxiety that has been stimulated in the brain stem and amygdala or limbic system. Over time, such empathic connections may help rewire the neural networks that, in the case of Barb, are tied to her intense anxiety, trauma, and possible abuse. Clients who have suffered severe trauma, neglect, and abuse need time to heal. Short-term therapy approaches are not as useful as long-term work with this client group.

As it turned out, Barb did reveal a long history of abuse and neglect after she felt safe enough in the therapy relationship. The clinical work could begin only after she felt protected in the relationship with the therapist. Winnicott (1971), an object relations theorist, refers to this technique as providing a holding environment. Neuroscientists would describe this process as the rewriting of neural networks, or neural plasticity (Cozolino, 2002).

There are multiple pathways to helping different clients establish a helpful therapeutic relationship. The models, theories, and paradigms discussed here will help lay the groundwork for effective practice.

BASIS OF PRACTICE

In my previous book, *Theory and Practice with Adolescents: An Applied Approach*, I presented the notion of a basis of practice with which to examine the empirical status of the concepts discussed in each chapter (McKenzie, 2008). Each topical area in this book includes a discussion of the basis of practice, whether in intuitive knowledge, practice wisdom, theoretical knowledge, or validated knowledge. The overall emphasis is on informed practice, or a range of empirical processes by which the clinician attempts to plan and carry out interventions and evaluate the successes or failures to determine whether they should continue to be used or should be modified. It is quite possible that an entirely different approach might be in order. Powers, Meenaghan, and Toomey (1985) refer to this process as practice-focused research. Their powerful argument is that there are different types of knowledge and a range of processes in which clinicians can examine, understand, and use it to help the clinical process.

Intuitive knowledge and common sense is the first and most basic type. All humans rely on common sense to function every day. It is essential for life. It is highly subjective.

Next is assumptive knowledge and practice wisdom. This type of knowledge is based on the clinician's clinical experience and the understanding that he or she has been able to acquire from that experience. It is not knowledge that an empirical process has necessarily validated. In other words, most clinicians have learned what works best for them.

Theoretical knowledge derives from the use of developmental and clinical theories. Clinicians use the hypotheses from such theories to help them develop their view of the practice situation and ultimately decide on a clinical approach. Every competent clinician should base his or her practice decisions on some form of practice theory. The process of deciding on one or several theories, using them in the clinical process, and evaluating the relative success of each is part of the development of practice wisdom. Clinicians should not apply theories randomly—nor should they adhere to theories if they are not working. In this sense, clinical practice is a research process.

The final form is validated knowledge, or knowledge that clinicians have gained through a more formalized and rigorous process of research. There has been relatively little validated knowledge about the clinical process. The clinical situation is a complex environment with multiple variables that are difficult to operationalize and measure. How does one fully capture the concept of transference? How is hope defined so that it can be measured and studied? These are challenging issues for clinical researchers and clinicians.

The theoretical and practice concepts in each chapter will be examined from the perspective of the four levels of research knowledge indicated in Powers, Meenaghan, and Toomey's (1985) text: assumptive practice knowledge, practice wisdom knowledge, theoretical practice knowledge, and validated practice knowledge.

Attachment theory encompasses all four levels of research knowledge. Human beings are intuitively drawn toward empathic connection with others, especially if they have been fortunate enough to establish some form of solid attunement in their own lives. That intuition leads clinicians toward a sense of practice knowledge once they have been able to develop a certain level of competence in their therapeutic work. Theories on attachment have been around for generations, lending credibility to the practice knowledge. Finally, recent research in attachment and neuroscience has lifted attachment theory to the level of validated practice knowledge (Ainsworth et al., 1978; Alliance of Psychoanalytic Organizations, 2006; Barber, 2000; Bowlby, 1969, 1973, 1980).

Object relations theory typically falls into the third level of research knowledge, theoretical practice knowledge. I use the word *typical* because there is a body of empirical knowledge from attachment and neuroscience theories that directly relates to object relations theory. The new *Psychodynamic Diagnostic Manual* (Alliance of Psychoanalytic Organizations, 2006) mentioned earlier devotes almost a third of text to recent empirical literature on these concepts. There is no question that object relations theory has solidly been in the first three areas of research knowledge for years. It is, however, becoming more and more validated through the research literature. Classic theoretical works from the likes of D. W. Winnicott (1965), Heinrich Racker (1968), and others are moving from the theoretical to the validated knowledge realm with the advent of such important literature.

Self-psychology has a firm footing in the area of theoretical knowledge. Although not validated through clinical research per se, the self-psychology concepts, like object relations before them, are gaining greater credibility from the recent attachment and neuroscience research studies (Greenspan & Shanker, 2006; Shevrin, 2006). The advancement of research in these key areas has helped join together so much of the previous theoretical literature with empirical and validated knowledge.

Rogerian theory and therapy is one of the early paradigms of the therapeutic relationship that has been empirically examined. Carl Rogers (1957) is noted for his rigorous research on the positive effect of empathy on the therapeutic relationship. In fact, this research is the main reason why Rogerian concepts and techniques have withstood the test of time. The therapeutic relationship is one of the few variables of the clinical process that seems to have been universally acknowledged as an effective element of practice (Prochaska & Norcross, 2003).

Neuroscience, even more so than attachment theory, sits squarely in the fourth area of research knowledge, validated knowledge. The study of the human brain continues to demonstrate that the other three levels of research knowledge—assumptive, practice, and theoretical—were correct. More texts examining how neuroscience informs clinical practice are coming forth (Cozolino, 2002; Siegel, 1999). This is an exciting time for clinical practitioners. What was previously considered an art form is becoming more and more validated as both a science and an art!

SUMMARY

This chapter has examined the major theories, models, and paradigms that will be used throughout the remainder of the text to explore the crucial aspects of understanding and managing the therapeutic relationship. Attachment, object relations, self-psychology, Rogerian, and neuroscience theories are invaluable, integrated resources in helping clinicians use emotions in the therapeutic process. Throughout the book, those implicit, intuitive, and elusive elements of the therapist-client relationship will be studied in depth to help integrate the theories and techniques so crucial to helping the client.

RECOMMENDED READINGS

Alliance of Psychoanalytic Organizations. (2006). *Psychodynamic diagnostic manual.* Silver Spring, MD: Author.

> Mentioned several times throughout the chapter and used for the remainder of the book, this monumental work elegantly elaborates on and integrates attachment and neuroscience theory with diagnostic clinical practice.

Cozolino, L. (2002). *The neuroscience of psychotherapy.* New York: Norton.

> This very interesting text is a masterpiece of knowledge that weaves neuroscience theory and research into the fabric of various psychotherapeutic models and modalities.

Elson, M. (1986). *Self psychology in clinical social work.* New York: Norton.

> Although a social work text, Elson's book does a solid job of elucidating the nature of the clinical relationship from the self-psychology perspective.

Gendlin, E. T. (1978). *Focusing.* New York: Everest House.

> Gendlin's original work on focusing is a helpful, practical guide for clinicians interested in accessing the inner emotions for treatment success.

Mitchell, S. A. (1988). *Relational concepts in psychoanalysis: An integration.* Cambridge, MA: Harvard University Press.

> This is Mitchell's wonderful contribution to examining the interactive relational aspects of the clinical relationship.

Ogden, T. (1982). *Projective identification and psychotherapeutic technique.* New York: Aronson.

> Ogden is renowned for his impeccable handling of the elusive concept of projective identification. He uses some very informative case examples to help tease out this complex principle.

Prochaska, J. O., & Norcross, J. C. (2003). *Systems of psychotherapy: A transtheo-retical analysis* (5th ed.). Pacific Grove, CA: Thomson Brooks/Cole.

Prochaska and Norcross provide a thorough and detailed examination of the research related to clinical practice.

Racker, H. (1968). *Transference and countertransference.* London: Hogarth Press.

Racker's work is little known but a classic piece of practical and theoretical literature for clinicians interested in countertransference.

Rogers, C. R. (1965). *Client-centered therapy.* Boston: Houghton-Mifflin.

This is the definitive Carl Rogers—it presents Rogers's major concepts as well as some of the empirical literature related to his principles.

Tansey, M. J., & Burke, W. F. (1989). *Understanding countertransference: From projective identification to empathy.* Mahwah, NJ: Analytic Press.

I used this text as one of many guides to explore the clinical literature related to countertransference. It is an invaluable source of historical reference on the subject.

Winnicott, D. W. (1965). *The maturational processes and the facilitating environ-ment.* New York: International Universities Press.

This is one of the most impressive works on object relations theory. One can truly grasp the essence of theoretical brilliance from reading Winnicott's original formulations.

OTHER RESOURCES

In treatment. (2008). New York: HBO.

This new series captures the trials and tribulations of an experienced psycho-therapist. Watch this show not for proper technique or ethical management but for a depiction of the emotional intensity of the clinical relationship.

http://www.focusing.org

The Web site of the Focusing Institute provides a solid example of the prin-ciples of Gendlin's concepts.

http://www.selfpsychology.com

The Self Psychology Page not only is a good reference for the works of Kohut but also provides some key training information.

http://www.sfn.org

The Web page of the Society for Neuroscience is a valuable source for up-to-date information on the current state of neuroscience theory and research.

Engagement and Assessment in the Therapeutic Relationship

ENGAGEMENT AND ATTACHMENT

Why does anyone enter into therapy? There is certainly not one simple answer to this question. Children and most adolescents are brought to therapy by their parents or coerced by important others in their lives (McKenzie, 2008). Many adults are mandated to attend therapy by a court order. However, the overwhelming majority of people choose to come to counseling for help.

Why would anyone seek out a stranger for help with deeply personal matters? How can people begin to trust a stranger with their most intimate thoughts, emotions, feelings, and problems? That is an intriguing question. Human beings are social animals, designed to emotionally attach to others for growth and survival (Ainsworth, Blehar, Waters, & Wall, 1978; Bowlby, 1969). The development of an internalized self is a complex process that can be understood from a variety of theoretical and empirical viewpoints: attachment theory, psychodynamic theory, cognitive development theory, behavioral development theory, systems theory, neuroscience theory, and so on. All of these are rich sources of information that help the clinician understand some of the possible ways in which a self is developed and internalized. But why does anyone seek out a complete stranger to discuss deeply personal matters?

There are several explanations for this paradoxical phenomenon. One of the most viable ones comes from Carl Rogers (1961), who discussed clients' cognitive dissonance as it relates to their sense of self. As people begin to have experiences in life that challenge, compromise, or conflict with their sense of self, they can become confused, anxious, ashamed, or angry—or they can experience various other complex thoughts and emotions. People usually seek comfort through the support of significant others in their lives, such as family, friends, peers, or colleagues. However, sometimes clients' issues are too intimate, vulnerable, embarrassing, shaming, or complex to trust to those who are close to them.

Professional therapy provides clients with an objective unbiased trained expert who can truly empathize with their plight without any personal entanglements. As does confessing to a priest, rabbi, or minister, the professional therapy relationship offers a private environment in which to emotionally heal. Unlike meeting with clergy, however, judgment is suspended in professional counseling, and it is fundamentally confidential. That type of special relationship is unique in today's world.

For most human beings, the primary attachment relationship helps cement a physical, emotional, and cognitive neurological network that generates a degree of trust in the world. Winnicott (1965) has described this as the holding environment. Symbolically and literally, it is this very same concept that helps facilitate engagement in virtually all clinical settings by providing a level of physical and emotional safety with which to engage in the therapeutic process. Therapists, however, are not primary caretakers in the same sense as those who attach to infants. Their work is much more complex in many ways because of the multilayered presentation of clients in treatment. The therapist's carefully attuned response to the initial anxiety about therapy for Barb, from chapter 1, is a good example of this approach. In other words, a more direct questioning of Barb's interest in therapy would ignore the obvious tension and anxiety that she was feeling.

Infants do not have language. Clients in therapy present a much more sophisticated communicative style. Words, tone of voice, vitality affects (Stern, 1985), body posture, style of dress, and other even subtler elements must be understood to be able to engage with clients and ultimately help resolve their problem. This is no easy task.

Recent advances in neuroscience research have discovered mirror neurons, which fire in response to highly specific relationship interactions:

> It is logical to assume that facial expressions, gestures, and posture of another will activate similar sensory-motor circuits in the observer. These motor systems, in turn, activate networks of emotion associated with such actions. Seeing a sad child makes us reflexively frown, tilt our heads, say "aawwhhhh," and feel sad with them. . . . In these and other ways, mirror neurons may help bridge the gap between sender and receiver, helping us understand one another and enhance the possibility of empathic attunement. . . . Our own internal state—generated via mirroring—can become our intuitive "theory" of the internal state of another. (Cozolino, 2002, pp. 185–186)

Until recently, the empathic process could not be defined by such precise neurological mechanisms. It seems clear from recent research that mirror neurons play a key role in the empathic identification that therapists use in engagement and ongoing work with clients.

David Wallin (2007), in his *Attachment in Psychotherapy*, also has emphasized the crucial importance of neuroscience in helping to understand the engagement process in treatment as it relates to early infancy:

> Facial expression and tone of voice, posture and gesture, the rhythms and contours of speech and behavior—these are the elements that compose what is essentially a medium of body to body communication. Such communication during infancy can be seen as a conversation between the baby's somatic/emotional self and the caregiver's somatic/emotional self—or, from a neuroscience perspective, as a "conversation between limbic systems." . . . The subject of this conversation is mainly the infant's internal states, the infant learns about herself and others: What are her own emotions and intentions? Will others recognize and attune to them? Will it "work" for her to take the initiative—independently or with the help of others—to attempt to affect her own internal states? (p. 119)

The engagement or assessment process in clinical work encompasses all these key factors. Trained therapists learn how to use them to develop an attuned, nonjudgmental relationship aimed to help clients resolve their difficulties. They also rely on these complex processes to begin to formulate an initial assessment of the client, one that should continually be modified and revised throughout the course of treatment.

Engagement and assessment are intimately tied together in the treatment situation. Once again, an example from early attachment helps illustrate this process. The primary caretaker engages with the infant through a variety of key attachment processes: vision, hearing, touch, speech, and so on. To regulate the infant's needs, the primary caretaker must be vigilant in recognizing and responding to the quality of the infant's functioning to adjust to his or her needs. If something seems wrong, that communication coming from the infant is not verbal but consists of other preverbal communications. The primary caretaker's mirror neurons are an especially crucial element in this interaction, enabling him or her to quickly assess and adjust to modify the attachment engagement process.

The clinical treatment situation is no different in principle. One major variation is that clients have verbal language, and verbal language becomes one of the main mechanisms by which engagement and assessment occur. Therapists use their knowledge, intuition, and mirror neurons to assess the extent to which the client is engaged, troubled, anxious, irritable, and so on. Verbal responses from the clinician are based on this assessment and aimed at helping to soothe clients and respond to their situation.

Case Examples: Judy

Several case examples will help to illustrate these principles. In my book *Theory and Practice with Adolescents: An Applied Approach* (McKenzie, 2008), I discussed the difficulty of engaging a complex young woman, Judy.

Judy came to see me for therapy when she was a junior in high school. Her parents brought her in for treatment because they were concerned about her physical and emotional withdrawal from the family. In addition, Judy's father gave me a novel that Judy was reading that gave him and his wife some concern. The novel was very dark, depressing, and sexual in content. Judy's parents were worried that their daughter was withdrawing into herself and becoming obsessed with evil and the pessimistic parts of life. They told me that when they spoke with Judy about coming to therapy she was very open to the idea.

I saw Judy individually, with occasional family meetings to review how therapy was going and keep her concerned parents in the loop. I wasn't sure what to expect when Judy came in alone for the first session. She appeared somewhat odd, disjointed, in both her physical appearance and her approach to conversation and interaction. One might characterize Judy as having a goth appearance—by that, I mean that she initially dressed primarily in black, with heavy black eye makeup, lipstick, and fingernail polish. Sometimes her hair was jet black, sometimes black and pink, sometimes all blue, and so on. She seemed not only shy in her demeanor but also a bit disorganized in her ability to communicate her thoughts and feelings. Her ideas were not delusional or odd, but her ability to accurately express those ideas seemed compromised. It was as if Judy were thinking and feeling a great deal about herself and her life but was having difficulty verbally expressing those thoughts and feelings.

The clinical sessions felt awkward, but it certainly appeared that Judy wanted to be there. She seemed pleasant and interested in discussing her thoughts and feelings. The problem for me was that there seemed to be a disconnect between what Judy openly expressed in session and my ability to respond to it empathically with words that fit for Judy. I wondered initially if she was suffering from the beginnings of some sort of psychotic thought disorder. She seemed to be highly intelligent, sensitive, and introspective. Her trouble appeared to have more to do with a sense of isolation, a sense that no one was able to understand her unique inner world or validate it for her. This was represented in therapy by an inability to clearly communicate those thoughts and emotions.

The awkwardness that I continued to experience with Judy was extremely troubling. Judy seemed so obviously handcuffed by her verbal ability. And yet it wasn't that she did not have a wide vocabulary or social sense. Judy's difficulty seemed to lie in her inability to put her complete complex emotional ideas into words. Her language proficiency was not sufficient to capture the full meaning of her experience. I realized that my task was to help her find a way to do just that.

There were many different ways I tried to help Judy feel better about herself. One of those was sharing some of my own experiences with emotional confusion in response to the confusion that Judy seemed to be expressing in her conversations in session. When Judy seemed to stumble in her ability to express a complete sense of her experience about something in her life, I would help her piece it together. I might share how that particular incident seemed reminiscent of something I had gone through in high school with friends, parents, or teachers. I would attempt to convey the complexities of emotion that I had experienced back then and how troublesome they had been for me. I would also share how isolated and alone that type of thinking could make one feel. I wanted her to realize that, although she might not have felt able to communicate her exact emotions regarding a particular experience, I could relate to it (McKenzie, 2008).

This case example is a wonderful illustration of how clinicians use a variety of processes to understand, engage, and assess clients. Judy presents with a particular challenge, a difficulty in using language to adequately express thoughts and emotions. These types of situations are probably more common than most therapists realize. In fact, clinicians must constantly rely on vicarious emotion, cognitive understanding, and recognition of the wide range of nonverbal communication to truly engage with clients. I was able to recognize that Judy needed help to feel less isolated and better able to function in her life. Because of her language deficit, I intuitively decided to offer, through self-disclosure, an empathic response aimed at resonating with her feelings. Judy's response to those interventions communicated relief and a sense of comfort about feeling less alone in her world. This is what empathic identification is all about—helping clients feel less alone with their thoughts and emotions and more connected and OK.

Engagement and assessment are intimately tied together in the treatment relationship. The ability to successfully attach to the client allows the clinician the opportunity to experience an authentic client. This authenticity can translate into assessment and diagnostic terminology. How might a clinician diagnose or assess Judy? Diagnosing adolescents is always a tricky proposition because they are in the middle of the developmental phase of identity formation. Their identity is not as static as that of a mature adult but is much more fluid and in process. Therefore, the developmental process itself should temper any diagnosis.

I experienced Judy as a bit depressed, confused, isolated, and insecure. For many adolescents, this is part of normal development. However, is Judy's experience more severe? Does it warrant a full-fledged diagnosis of major depression? Probably not. Does it warrant a diagnosis of dysthymia, a chronic form of mild depression? Probably not. However, Judy's diagnosis probably should include some form of a depressive disorder. Because she was *adjusting* to her adolescent identity formation, I believed that the DSM IV-TR diagnosis of adjustment disorder 309.28, with mixed anxiety and depression, was in order.

For Judy, her diagnostic makeup suggests that she is struggling with her identity, a sense of isolation, and some intermittent sadness. The therapy relationship will help her mitigate that difficulty over time. In the meantime, an adjustment disorder diagnosis helps guide clinicians in their work with her. This means that Judy is struggling to feel comfortable with her sense of self as she adjusts to adolescence. I would say that Judy's struggle is more pronounced than that of most adolescents, which is what has led her to therapy. In a safe, empathic therapeutic environment, Judy can find a meaningful sense of self that is understood and validated in the therapeutic relationship.

Mr. D

Mr. D is a forty-four-year-old sales executive who presented with mild depression and dissatisfaction with his present position. Throughout his childhood, he had felt pushed by his family to succeed for them rather than to find his own identity and sense of value. He used the sessions to explore exactly what he wanted to do in his professional life. The worker found himself feeling an uneasiness in the sessions with Mr. D. The content seemed meaningful to Mr. D., but the worker felt a compelling sense of ineptness and social awkwardness with this client. The worker regrettably continued his work with Mr. D. The worker almost dreaded the sessions, and yet he knew that there must be something he was missing (McKenzie, 1999).

This case will be revisited in subsequent chapters, but I introduce it here to highlight some of the subtler and challenging aspects of the engagement process. Feelings such as those experienced in the engagement process with Mr. D are not at all unusual. In fact, they become the elements through which the clinician is able to not only engage clients but also understand, assess, and work with them.

Mr. D elicited a degree of anxiety and uncertainty in the clinician from the onset of therapy. What might this signal from an engagement or assessment standpoint? Perhaps Mr. D is himself anxious or even uncertain to some extent. The therapist can use this cue both to help foster engagement and to illuminate possible diagnostic information. Even though Mr. D does not clearly indicate that he is anxious, the internal state of the therapist could be a fairly strong indicator of that fact. This could be a simple example of traditional countertransference or a more complex aspect of the relational matrix mentioned previously.

The therapist can begin to use more soothing interventions to help Mr. D feel less anxious. This type of interaction is very similar to what a caretaker might do for an anxious or troubled infant. Using a reassuring, soothing, or comforting tone of voice with Mr. D will probably help him recognize that the clinician not only feels and understands his anxiety but also is able to respond in a way that can help. This type of therapeutic intervention oftentimes happens intuitively, in much the same way that an empathic caretaker intuitively responds to an infant.

Although Mr. D's therapist responded in an empathic manner, the anxiety and awkwardness of the interaction continued to a certain extent. From a diagnostic standpoint, this usually signals that the client has a deeper underlying difficulty. In other words, the emotions experienced in the first sessions are not related simply to coming to therapy; they may be a strong clue to the presenting problem or even an underlying character difficulty.

THE TREATMENT PLAN

Successful clinical treatment, like successful human relationships in general, is doubtful without attuned and emotionally healthy attachments. Unfortunately, the constraints of many social service organizations, mental health agencies, and even private practices require clinicians to develop treatment plans that may run counter to the notion of developing an empathic working relationship with clients. Concepts like SOAP—subjective, objective, assessment, plan—are an example of the type of treatment plan required by many organizations, especially insurance companies. In addition, most of these same settings require that the clinician gather extensive factual and demographic information from the client in the first session.

How does the clinician establish a working alliance with the client while having to gather factual information and document the clinical session in primarily behavioral terms? This is not an easy task. The simple process of asking personal questions of the client before an empathic relationship has been established can derail or even end the clinical situation before it has even begun. It is important to remember how the client might feel or react. Keeping that simple premise foremost in the clinician's mind is essential.

Here are some other helpful suggestions. Having the client fill out an informational sheet before the first session has begun can help distance that process from the experience of engaging with the clinician. Informing the client that this type of information is part of agency policy and necessary to start the treatment process also helps.

Another useful way to separate this process from the clinical relationship is to do it immediately in the very first session. Let the client know that first you need to ask some required questions and gather some information that will be helpful in therapy. Explain that this might feel a bit awkward because the two of you have just met and that some of the questions are quite personal. However, presenting the information gathering in this way can help remove it from the more personal process of building the therapeutic relationship through conversation.

Another major difficulty in the treatment plan scenario is developing a series of behavioral goals for the client when the actual presenting concern is quite complex. Reducing the human experience to concrete behavioral terminology is useful for documentation purposes, but it does not always capture the emotional life of a client. I certainly believe that many problems that clients describe can be listed as problems tied to interventions and goals. However, many cannot. The clinical dilemma is how to accomplish the requirements of the organization while doing good therapeutic work with the client. Both of these requirements are essential and legitimate, but to work successfully with clients, a therapeutic relationship must be established (Barber, 2000).

Most clinicians successfully adjust to these requirements, but the beginning intern or professional can have some problems with it. A helpful rule of thumb is to approach this situation as two separate tasks. Information gathering and objective treatment planning is a primarily concrete and behavioral exercise. Engaging the client is much more relational, subtle, and complex.

The two cases discussed here required two very different treatment plans. Judy was not able to identify specific behavioral goals for her therapeutic work. In fact, she was not entirely sure what she needed, except that it felt good to be able to be understood and feel less isolated by being in counseling. From a behavioral standpoint, the initial treatment plan might simply state that a goal for Judy is to feel less anxious and isolated by identifying and discussing her thoughts, feelings, and emotions in weekly therapy sessions. Over time, Judy and her therapist should be able to identify specific areas of insecurity, or even triggers from her daily life that they can address in counseling. The actual session work with Judy, however, would most likely consist of helping elicit thoughts, emotions, and understanding related to her life and identity formation.

Mr. D would probably require a much more concretized treatment plan. For example, Mr. D would want to know in short order exactly what he wants in life. Should he remain in the business world? Should he pursue education in another field? Should he retire early and start his own business? These are the types of questions to which Mr. D would need speedy answers in his therapy.

In contrast, the therapy with Mr. D was successful only once he was able to move beyond specific goals and gain insight into some of the reasons he was so unsettled about his future. This does not mean that Mr. D needed to undergo long-term psychotherapy. It did mean that, to continue with his life on a happier path, he needed to have some insight into why he seemed to choose jobs that were continually dissatisfying.

BASIS OF PRACTICE

The engagement aspect of the clinical relationship has reached the upper level of research knowledge, validated knowledge (Baldwin, Wampold, & Imel, 2007; Dozier & Kobak, 1992; Gallese, 2001; Lambert & Barley, 2001; Schachner, Shauer, & Mikulincer, 2005). Probably since the beginning of human interaction, there has been an intuitive sense that attachment and empathy are crucial for successful relationships and development in general. Practice and theoretical knowledge on this subject has existed for many decades (Racker, 1968; Rogers, 1965; Searles, 1979; Stern, 1985; Winnicott, 1965). Only recently has there been research that indicates the validity of attachment as a necessary condition for an engaged therapeutic relationship. Various scholars have written extensively on the empirical effectiveness of psychotherapy in patient outcomes (Barber, 2000; Hubble, Duncan, & Miller, 1999; Leichsenring & Rabung, 2008). There is no doubt that, regardless of the problem or therapeutic approach used, success in treatment depends on an engaged therapeutic relationship derived from attachment theories.

SUMMARY

Engagement and assessment are integrally connected in the therapeutic process. To engage with clients, the clinician must be able to empathically connect with them on the verbal and nonverbal levels. Several theories help clinicians understand this process, including attachment, client-centered, and neuroscience paradigms. Actual case examples are the most practical ways to illustrate and understand this phenomenon. Each client will require his or her own unique treatment plan based on the situation at hand and his or her ability to communicate and gain insight into problems. It is the therapist's responsibility to connect in a way that best facilitates this crucial process.

RECOMMENDED READINGS

Lambert, M., & Barley, D. (2001). Research summary on the therapeutic relationship and psychotherapy outcome. *Psychotherapy, 38*(4), 357–361.

This important research review thoroughly covers the material presented in chapter 2 of this book at the validated knowledge level.

Rogers, C. R. (1961). *On becoming a person.* Boston: Houghton-Mifflin.

Many consider Rogers's work the quintessential text on the importance of empathy in successful clinical work and human relationships. He combines thoughtful clinical material with empirical research to present his compelling, time-tested arguments.

Wallin, David J. (2007). *Attachment in psychotherapy.* New York: Guilford Press.

This text presents cutting-edge research and insightful material on the crucial importance of attachment in the development and successful resolution of issues in the therapeutic relationship.

OTHER RESOURCES

In treatment. (2008). New York: HBO.

Recommended in chapter 1, this series is an excellent practical example of what should and should not be done to establish a solid therapeutic alliance.

Spielberg, S. (Producer & Director). (1982). *E.T.: The extra-terrestrial* [Motion picture]. United States: Amblin Entertainment.

Certainly a classic film by any standards, *E.T.* also helps any clinician better understand the intuitive necessity of empathic identification and attachment.

http://www.focusing.org

Gendlin's Web site for the Focusing Institute provides a solid example of the necessity of personal awareness as a prerequisite for successful engagement in clinical work.

The Intersubjective Realm

Perhaps the most valuable but challenging aspect of clinical work is the understanding and use of the emotional aspects of the intersubjective realm in the therapeutic relationship. This concept has been traditionally known as the transference-countertransference continuum. The ability not only to understand the complex emotional elements of the therapist-client relationship but also to use them effectively in treatment is one of the most important hallmarks of clinical work. This chapter reviews the historical underpinnings of this phenomenon and discusses specific techniques crucial to working with clients in all forms of therapy.

TRANSFERENCE

Sigmund Freud discovered and developed the concept of transference during his work with analytic patients in the late nineteenth and early twentieth centuries. In psychoanalysis, a patient free associates, meaning that the therapist encourages them to say whatever comes to mind. The analyst must be a blank screen, that is, not intrude or gratify the patient in any way that may interfere in his or her ability to free associate. One of Freud's most famous patients, Anna O., reached a point in her analysis at which she found it difficult and even refused to continue to free associate. Freud recognized this as a major form of resistance to the treatment and focused his efforts on encouraging her to continue to free associate. Over time, Anna O. resumed free association but with a new twist in content and emotion. She focused almost exclusively on the relationship with Freud, which baffled him. He felt that he must get her to resume discussing her own issues and not her relationship with or fantasies about him. Anna O., however, refused to do much else but focus on her relationship with Freud. She discussed her feelings, wishes, hopes, and dreams about him. Freud eventually began to understand and realize that this was a very important issue for her. Freud hypothesized that perhaps Anna O. was in fact discussing issues in her own life history—important relationships, emotions, fears, wishes—disguised unconsciously as symbolic issues with Freud. In other words, she might not have felt such things about Freud (whom she presumably did not know much about) but was actually transferring onto him her own neurotic concerns. As Freud was able to decipher this symbolism and interpret it to Anna O., she was able to have insight not only into her relationship with Freud but also into the meanings of those symbolic interactions in her past and present life. Anna O.'s improvement in analysis was the proof that Freud had stumbled on a remarkable discovery not only about analysis but also human nature in general (McKenzie, 2008).

COUNTERTRANSFERENCE

Freud's initial formulation became the primary theoretical premise from which all further work on the therapeutic relationship evolved. He went on to develop the theory of countertransference, which countless clinicians and theorists have expanded and modified over the past hundred years.

The history of the predominant theoretical viewpoints on countertransference theory has evolved from the classical to the totalist and specialist positions over the past century (Tansey & Burke, 1989). Freud (1912) created the classical stance when he recommended that the physician "put aside all his feelings" to be fully attentive to the patient's free associations (Freud, 1912). This stance may have had more to do with the development of transference theory than any negation of the importance of countertransference. Several times throughout his writing, he mentioned the inevitable importance of paying close attention to the physician's unconscious as important information about the patient (Tansey & Burke, 1989). Ironically, this represented the beginnings of the classical versus totalist debate.

Over the following thirty years, the debate continued on the extent to which the therapist should focus on and use his or her own emotional processes (conscious and unconscious) in the treatment relationship. Theorists examined the effect and inevitability of the analyst's personality on the therapeutic situation (Balint & Balint, 1939; Klauber, 1968). Most of them concluded that, although there certainly was inevitable personal influence, that could be minimized by adhering to strict analytic technique. Others proposed that the analyst engage in a type of identification with the patient to truly understand his or her emotional life (Fliess, 1942).

Melanie Klein posited the first notable shift away from the classical position on countertransference. Her object relations theory described the process of projective identification: a developmental ego defense that, when combined with splitting (another defense), helped explain and normalize many of the intense emotional reactions that therapists experience in relationship with their clients (Klein, 1946). Others elaborated on this phenomenon, which led to the development of what has been called the totalist view of countertransference (Giovacchini, 1981; Heimann, 1950; Winnicott, 1949). The totalist position suggests that the conscious and unconscious emotional representations of therapists and clients continually intermingle with each other in therapist-client interactions. This leads to the notion of a continuum, with the client's issues on one side represented as projective identifications and the therapist's issues on the other represented as their own countertransference contributions. It can become quite difficult to ascertain whose emotional issues and conflicts, client's or therapist's, are most dominant in the interaction. The totalist position emphasizes the importance of consistent self-awareness as part and parcel of intervention on the part of the therapist to best serve the client.

The most notable and comprehensive theorist of the totalist countertransference camp was Heinrich Racker. His elaborate theory distinguished several different types of countertransference, most notably concordant and complimentary identifications (Racker, 1968). Racker acknowledged inevitable personal influences, which he called nonneurotic countertransference, as well as countertransferences, which derived from emotional conflicts. Concordant identifications consisted of the therapist's empathic feelings and responses to clients. Complimentary identifications represented the compelling emotional reactions that resulted from the unconscious acceptance of the client's projective identifications or disavowed emotional representations from the past. It became the therapist's task to successfully mediate between the two processes, some more compelling (positions) and others more benign (thoughts). This is the definitive totalist position, one that recognizes the ongoing mutually interactive and constructed process in the clinical relationship.

The specialist position has evolved to elaborate on the types and manner in which countertransference can be recognized and handled within the therapeutic relationship. Some have expanded the role of empathy to include the therapist's identification process (Tansey & Burke, 1989). Others write about a process of counteridentification stimulated by the client's projective identifications (Grinberg, 1962).

In a more radical stance, some theorists have argued that acknowledging intense primitive love for the client—and with more disturbed cases, even physical touch—may be therapeutic in some cases (Little, 1981; Searles, 1979). The position is that these intense emotional reactions (therapist's thoughts and feelings) are diagnostic indicators of the client's pathology and a clue to unresolved emotional issues with the therapist as a symbolic representation of important earlier relationships with caretakers. The inevitability of experiencing such phenomena in treatment enables therapists to better understand the client, and themselves, and provides the opportunity for more effective treatment (McKenzie, 1999).

Most recently, advances in attachment theory and neuroscience, especially contributions from the *Psychodynamic Diagnostic Manual* (Alliance of Psychoanalytic Organizations, 2006), have helped clinicians deepen their understanding of the physiological aspects of this relational concept, which has led to a greater ability to assess, intervene in, and facilitate the therapeutic treatment process.

One of the most useful ways for understanding this concept is through a more thorough discussion of Heinrich Racker's clinical validation method. That method helped clinicians systemically identify, understand, and more effectively work with intense and disruptive emotional experiences (Racker, 1968). Although somewhat linear in its description and depiction of the countertransference interaction, Racker's model was an innovative step in further elaborating countertransference work. He introduced the notion of working models of self and other, as well as the ways successful examination, understanding, and use of this information could benefit the therapeutic relationship.

Racker's method goes something like this: When clinicians experience intense countertransference reactions, those invariably interfere in the ability to stay engaged with the client. This can take the form of anxiety, boredom, anger, and a compelling inability to stay connected with the client, among many others. Sleep reaction (e.g., a compelling, uncontrollable urge to fall asleep during a clinical session when the therapist is not drowsy) is a good example of this phenomenon, as well. There is something happening in the therapeutic relationship that somehow is creating an impasse.

Racker postulated that, when this happens, there is some type of emotional stimulus from either the client or the therapist that disrupts the ability of the therapist to stay empathically attuned. He believed that one way to help resolve this dilemma was to identify the source of this distress, thereby relieving the conflict through awareness and insight. Racker (1968) believed that this could be accomplished through a careful examination of the working models of self and other.

What exactly are these working models? They are the sum total of the cognitive, emotional, and experiential memories of the history of the therapist and client. Racker, like Freud, believed that it was essential for clinicians to have a thorough understanding of their developmental history, as well as their identity, life history, and intellectual interests—in short, as much understanding as possible of the whole person.

Likewise, clinicians should develop a similar, though not as elaborate, working model of the client. This comes from a careful, attentive, and empathic connection and history with the client. Not all therapy situations reach this type of intimacy, but many do, even in short-term work.

How are the working models of self and other used in an impasse, like that described earlier? When clinicians experience emotions that are interfering in the therapeutic process, Racker would say that they must examine their own working model of self to ascertain whether there are sources of emotional conflict stimulated by a client's material (e.g., communications and history) or relationship that triggers, to the extent that it might inhibit clinicians' ability to stay empathically attuned. Such situations happen quite frequently, but clinicians do not always understand them as emanating from an inner emotional source.

On careful introspection and examination, troubled clinicians may identify that the source of their distress and distance comes from their own emotional conflicts, developmental history, and so on. If these insights are accurate, in Racker's view, the clinicians will gain insight and experience a sense of relief; an escape from debilitating thoughts, sensations, or emotions; and a renewed ability to reengage in the therapeutic process with the client. This validation frees therapists to refocus their attention, unencumbered by their own emotional conflict.

The same process is true in using the working model of the client. For example, after a thorough examination of a clinician's own working model of self—which should always be the first step in this process—the clinician can turn his or her attention to the client. The therapist's examination of his or her understanding of the client's developmental history, emotional conflicts, attachments, and object relations might give the therapist insight as to how and why the impasse is related to the client's relationships. Should this insight prove true to the clinician, the clinician will experience relief, insight, and a renewed ability to engage in the therapeutic process.

There is something not quite complete in this process as defined by Racker. The therapeutic interaction is not simply two dimensional or linear; it is relational and interactive. I do not believe that a clear-cut distinction between therapist and client can be made in exploring the etiology of an impasse. The exploration must be relational and interactive; both parties must contribute.

Many consider Racker's position to be the essence of what has come to be called the totalist position. In other words, countertransference is not only an ongoing process but also a diagnostic tool for understanding the subtle and overt emotional contributions of both the therapist and the client to the therapeutic process. This is a far cry from Freud's warning to clinicians to identify and eliminate their emotional proclivities.

RELATIONAL MODEL

Relational clinicians such as Mitchell (1988) have recognized that the therapeutic relationship constantly intermingles with the emotional needs of both the therapist and the client. Besides whatever developmental or historical information either party brings into the therapeutic setting, there is also a very real relationship that forms on the basis of the unique contributions of the client and the therapist. According to relational clinicians, to be completely helpful, honest, and ethical in working with all clients, the very real aspects of the present therapeutic encounter must be taken into consideration to help the client and the therapist grow from the experience.

Hopefully, the clinician working from a relational model is much more emotionally aware of one's own developmental history and is far more capable than the client of in-depth introspection in the therapeutic encounter (Mitchell, 1988). This approach differs substantially from the Racker model in its emphasis on the ongoing interactional relationship between the therapist and the client and, more important, how those interactions affect the entire therapeutic process.

PRACTICE TEMPLATE: ATTACHMENT AND
NEUROSCIENCE THEORIES

I have been intrigued for several years by the notion that all clinicians, from the novice to the most experienced, work from an internalized template that contains a range and repertoire of knowledge, emotions, and experiences that form the basis of their professional self. That self is the sum total of professional education, practice experiences, life experiences, emotional reactions, and residue from work as clinicians. This professional template starts out quite small and initially may be more conscious than intuitive, but eventually it forms the basis of our practice wisdom and confidence as therapists.

The recent advances in neuroscience and attachment theory research validate this assumption. All human beings are prewired to attach to primary caretakers. Attachment research by Bowlby (1969), Ainsworth, Blehar, Waters, and Wall (1978), and even Mahler, Pine and Bergman (1975) seem to clearly indicate the innate human need for others to survive not only emotionally but also physically. Neuroscience theory and research has discovered that human infants are born with mirror neurons, which enable them to anticipate the actions and intentions of caretakers before caretakers actually carry out certain behaviors. This means that human beings are prewired for empathy. Assuming all goes well in early attachment relationships, this ability will continue to develop a sense of trust and comfort in interacting with others in the world. If life circumstances are not quite good enough, the individual may not be as adept in negotiating relationships or life circumstances in general (Winnicott, 1965). Such individuals may be in greater need of guidance, structure, and help in life (Cozolino, 2002).

Another interesting contribution of neuroscience is the notion that neural networks in the brain contain all experience. The more these life experiences contain elements of cognition, emotion, and experience, the more effective the neural networks will be in helping individuals negotiate life's experiences and cope in times of stress. This complex neural network integrates electrical signals and activity from a variety of the areas of the brain that are crucial to comprehensive life functioning. Those people who have developed more integrated and sophisticated neural networks tend to manage life's challenges in more productive ways (Cozolino, 2002).

I would argue, from a neurological standpoint, that the practice template is the result of many years of comprehensive clinical experience that has helped seasoned clinicians intuitively draw from a sophisticated and complex neural network based on the variety of cognitive, emotional, and experiential aspects of their professional career. Novice clinicians do not have this ability because they haven't had the benefit of the many years of therapeutic successes and failures that have shaped the neural network of the practice template. That process takes time and hard work, just like any other success in life.

What does this have to do with a contemporary view of countertransference? All the models discussed here are elements of the evolving process of a practice template. Each clinician forms his or her own template based on the specific type of education and experience he or she has encountered in a professional career. Therefore, each template is different and perhaps more or less effective in any given clinical situation.

Case Example: Susan

The material covered here is complex and difficult to comprehend and applies if the clinician doesn't have a good amount of practice experience. The following case example illustrates the concepts discussed in a more practical application. It will also illustrate the ongoing contributions of both therapist and client in the clinical relationship, as well as what types of interventions can be used to further the work.

Susan has been in therapy with the clinician for several years. The presenting concern centered on dissatisfaction with her marriage to an apparently narcissistic, alcoholic, abusive man. The core of much of the work focused on Susan's fragile sense of self, poor body image, and overall sense of emotional isolation. Susan was convinced—despite any opinions to the contrary from her husband, peers, or the clinician—that she was ugly and would never feel pretty or be seen as beautiful by any man. This theme was continuous, an ongoing focus of the therapeutic relationship. Susan exhibited what might be labeled features of borderline personality organization.

During one session several weeks into treatment, Susan was discussing some rather vague concerns regarding her job, children, husband, and so on. Quite spontaneously, the clinician found himself struck by Susan's beauty. In fact, he was surprised to be thinking and feeling that Susan was perhaps the most beautiful woman he had ever seen. This was puzzling, because, subjectively, the worker did not find Susan to be extremely attractive. He also realized that his reaction was excessive, not like him, and made him feel quite anxious.

The clinician decided to use the clinical validation method to examine his own emotional reactions. Through exploring his own working model of self, the worker was not able to identify any material, conflicts, or themes that could help explain or alleviate his intense reaction. However, on exploring his internal working model of Susan, the clinician was able to retrieve a crucial piece of object relations issues from her childhood.

Susan experienced her parents as predominantly critical and withholding. In her early childhood, however, Susan remembered her father giving her baths and telling her she was pretty, which helped generate a feeling of true specialness, beauty, and importance. This special feeling stopped abruptly when Susan entered puberty and began to physically look more like a young woman than a child. Susan remembered her father refusing to give her baths, and in addition, drastically altering his positive behavior and treatment of her, which from that point on she experienced as distant and critical.

DISCUSSION

The retrieval of this memory of Susan's through the working model of the client enabled the clinician to recognize that his strong emotional reactions might be a reenactment of Susan's earlier life with her father. The idea that, in fact, his feelings were perhaps not just reenactments of the past but also the basis of a corrective emotional experience crucial to the repair of Susan's poor self-image immediately reduced the intensity of the clinician's experience. The insight was emotionally and physically relieving, and it allowed the practitioner to reengage with Susan with a greater understanding of her pain, life experience, and present need. The clinician was, in fact, responding to Susan's great need to recapture her positive sense of self and the beautiful self-image that had been lost in childhood. The compelling experience of Susan's beauty occurred because of the clinician's empathic ability to be attuned to her need to feel loved and special.

The clinician did not share this experience or insight directly with Susan; he used it to help him work with her to develop a greater sense of her own beauty and self-image. The clinician helped Susan experience a positive sense of herself in the relationship with him, which she could then experience with others in her world.

The apparently intuitive or even unconscious manner in which the clinician was able to be empathically attuned and experience Susan's needs can be explained by concepts from neuroscience. Cozolino (2002), in his remarkable book *The Neuroscience of Psychotherapy*, discusses the role and types of language utilized in development and psychotherapy:

> There appear to be at least three levels of language functioning accessed during psychotherapy. There is reflexive social language, an internal dialogue, and a language of self-reflection. *Reflexive social language* is a stream of words that function primarily in the maintenance of ongoing social communication and relatedness.

> As primate groups grew larger, reflexive social language most likely evolved from social grooming and hand-gestures (Dunbar, 1996; Rizzolatti & Arbib, 1998). This form of language mirrors the external interpersonal world and provides a matrix for ongoing communication with others. Unconscious reflexes and learned reactions in response to social situations and constraints "lubricate" our interpersonal relationships. Most of us experience this whenever we find ourselves automatically saying something positive to avoid or reduce tension.

> We are all aware of the voices we hear and the conversations we carry on within us as we struggle with the weighty issues of our lives or even decide where to go for dinner. This *internal dialogue*, guiding (or being guided by) our thoughts and behaviors, often departs from what we say socially. This level of language is also primarily reflexive and may have evolved on a separate track from social language, allowing for survival-enhancing deception. These two levels of language are like over-learned motor skills that usually serve as mechanisms to maintain preexisting attitudes, behaviors, and feelings. Most of our ongoing verbal production is habitual and continues to keep us in the mode *in which we have been shaped* [italics added]. We hear in our heads the supportive or critical voices of our parents, and we speak the language of our group. Like reflexive social language, internal dialogue is based upon semantic routines and habits that reflect our thoughts, behaviors, and social presentation.

Much of therapy consists of examining and attempting to understand reflexive social language and internal dialogue. This process expands perspective on many aspects of the *unconscious aspects of the self* [italics added]. In therapy, a *language of self-reflection* is either enhanced or created for the first time. (pp. 36–37)

Although lengthy, this invaluable quote from Cozolino lends some important insights to the work with Susan. The ability of the clinician to pick up on Susan's early childhood dispositions regarding her self-image and self-esteem can be understood as empathic mirroring. Susan's language, expression, and posture, combined with the historical content regarding her relationship with her father, could lead to the practitioner's countertransference response and subsequent empathic shift.

The experience contained the emotional expression of Susan's early sense of beauty and the admiration she received from her father while simultaneously causing the therapist to feel a sense of anxiety and tendency to distance as her father did. This is not difficult to understand from the standpoint of neuroscience, as Cozolino has described. Language and communication takes many forms and is constantly expressed in a variety of ways, including formal language. The therapeutic encounter is devoted to enlarging the opportunity to receive and understand many forms of communication from early childhood origins to present circumstances.

MANIFEST AND LATENT CONTENT

In the clinical experience, as in life, there are manifest and latent communications. Manifest communications are the literal words, syntax, and communication that emanates from the speaker. For example, a client concerned about her job will speak words that describe the particular situation, people, and circumstances, and perhaps even some feelings associated with the problem. In addition, however, there will be communication beyond the literal words—symbolic, indirect, conscious, or unconscious—that alludes to deeper meaning. The classic Freudian slip is a good example of this type of communication. However, the skilled clinician can be trained to listen to both levels of communication, manifest and latent, as they relate to the presenting concern and to the client's developmental history. Thematic communication of this nature can form a basis of core understanding regarding the client's life, attachment, developmental history, and many key elements so integral to helping the clinician facilitate a therapeutic relationship. Clinicians should combine understanding and working with manifest and latent communication with other therapeutic skills and understanding, such as the wide range of countertransference concepts already discussed. These are all part of the practice template.

Case Example: Mr. D Revisited

I introduced Mr. D's case example in chapter 2 to illustrate some of the subtle difficulties inherent in the engagement process of clinical work. In that case, the clinician was experiencing an uneasiness, ineptness, and feeling of awkwardness with Mr. D.

In examining his own working model of self, the worker was unable to identify any aspects of conflicted or even idiosyncratic self that substantially contributed to his uncomfortable feelings. In examining the working model of Mr. D, the clinician was still unable to ascertain any themes or object relation scenarios that could be understood as projective identification or complimentary identification. The worker regrettably continued his work with Mr. D, almost dreading the sessions and knowing that he must have been missing something. Several weeks later, Mr. D was discussing what he felt to be his greatest accomplishments. The worker asked almost nonchalantly what Mr. D felt were some of the most trying or troublesome aspects of his personality. Without a moment's hesitation, Mr. D said that, all of his life, especially in childhood, he had felt inept and uncomfortable in social situations, especially with peers. He had always felt awkward, and he frequently avoided such situations. The worker almost immediately experienced a sense of emotional relief as he realized the reenactment that had been taking place throughout so much of their work together. The therapist had been feeling the same type of anxiety and awkwardness as Mr. D. This experiential insight allowed the worker to reconnect with Mr. D in a more meaningful way (McKenzie, 1999).

DISCUSSION

The clinician's awareness of Mr. D's vulnerable sense of self throughout his development enabled him to better understand Mr. D's relationships in virtually all areas of his life. That kind of insight becomes a tool through which the clinician can approach all future conversation and intervention planning in sessions. Knowing that Mr. D is unsure of himself and uncertain in his identity forms the basis of all future work. In fact, one might argue that the resolution of Mr. D's complaints hinges on the extent to which he can resolve those concerns. Carefully timed empathic interventions that are based on the knowledge of Mr. D's insecurity can help modify his difficulties in life by restoring confidence.

This does not mean that the clinician cannot use a therapeutic model such as cognitive behavioral therapy or solution-focused therapy to center on specific concrete problems with measureable goals and outcomes. It means that, for those outcomes to be attained, the astute therapist must take into account the underlying personal characteristics that will invariably disrupt, interfere, or sidetrack the process.

This is the essential value of understanding and using the concepts discussed in this chapter. Although essentially psychodynamic in origin, they have integral utility in all forms of clinical practice, be they short or long term in nature. The extent to which these intricate concepts apply to the therapeutic relationship depends on each client and his or her unique development. The less conflicted the client is, the less intense the therapeutic relationship issues will be and the less they will enter into and complicate clinical work. However, clinicians still should be ever vigilant for intense emotional issues such as those discussed here.

RELATIONAL WORK

Contemporary relational theorists emphasize the importance of recognizing a continual real relationship that develops in all clinical work. There are elements of the client's transference, the therapist's countertransference, and the interplay and development of a new real relationship shaped by the unique configuration of each participant (Mitchell, 1988).

Racker's countertransference working models of self and other capture a good deal of relational thrust but do not fully elaborate on the integrative elements of the combined real relationships between client and therapist. For example, some people simply hit it off or get along better than others. Sometimes the very real common interests of clients and their therapists help form a bond that is quite different from those not sharing similar interests. In addition, one might argue that sharing common interests can interfere with or be a detriment to the successful development of a therapeutic alliance. Mutual blind spots might develop, for instance, between a client and a therapist who share the same religion, political beliefs, gender, race, and so on. Similar worldviews can potentially bond or blind therapist and client. However, clients and therapists with disparate viewpoints and interests can also interfere with the development of a secure therapeutic relationship. There is no hard-and-fast rule.

From a relational perspective, it is important to recognize that there are myriad interactional possibilities based on the unique qualities of therapist and client. Only then can the therapist attempt to form a successful therapeutic relationship. Turning a blind eye to these crucial concepts and factors is problematic in therapy and in life.

SPONTANEOUS SELF-DISCLOSURE

Joseph Palumbo (1983), in his article "Spontaneous Self Disclosures in Psychotherapy," discusses the intuitive ways clinicians respond to clients' repressed emotions by impulsively emoting in the session. Impulsively emoting means expressing emotions without censorship or prior intent. Before the advent of neuroscience and the discovery of mirror neurons, Palumbo's article might have been dismissed as unscientific and entirely theoretical in its premise. Palumbo posits that, in certain therapeutic relationships, clinicians may find themselves not only experiencing but actually expressing emotions that are intimately tied to the client's experience. The strong therapeutic attachment and empathic ability of therapists allows them to experience the client's emotion and in many cases spontaneously express that emotion in session.

From the standpoint of neuroscience, attuned clinicians use their mirror neurons to anticipate the emotional state of the client and expressing it to them in session. There is nothing magical about this process—it has its origins in early attachment, when being attuned is essential to healthy emotional development. In fact, one might argue that a phenomenon such as spontaneous self-disclosure is one of the many reparative elements in the skilled application of psychotherapy (Cozolino, 2002). One must be careful however, that self-disclosures of emotion are genuinely attuned to the client and not self-serving, or springing from the clinician's unexamined needs.

BASIS OF PRACTICE

The concepts covered in this chapter are quite complex and highly relevant to the successful understanding and management of the clinical relationship in psychotherapy. For more than a century, clinicians have intuitively understood the importance of concepts such as transference, countertransference, manifest and latent content, and the unconscious as integral elements in successful outcomes of the therapeutic process. In addition, countless case studies have documented the practice wisdom of recognizing and using such complex variables in treatment. Many theorists mentioned in this chapter have written extensively on this important subject.

The first three levels of research knowledge—intuitive, assumptive, and theoretical—have existed for quite some time (Tansey & Burke, 1989). Validated knowledge has been developing over the past few years (Alliance of Psychoanalytic Organizations, 2006; Cozolino, 2002; Lyons-Ruth & Boston Change Process Study Group, 2001). In particular, recent advances in neuroscience clearly indicate the neurological mechanism from early infancy that plays a crucial part in attachment and the ability to form relationships throughout life and relate in empathic ways to others. It is this last piece of information that is so valuable to the clinician in recognizing and responding to the troubled emotions of clients in therapy (Barber, 2000; Cozolino, 2006; Leichsenring & Rabung, 2008).

SUMMARY

This chapter is the heart of the entire text. Understanding and managing the therapeutic relationship is the fundamental core of all clinical work, regardless of the theoretical orientation of the clinician or the treatment modality. An examination of the historical literature from Freud (1912) to Racker (1968), and from Mitchell (1988) to Wallin (2007), combined with an examination of the contributions of contemporary neuroscience, helps shape a comprehensive understanding and approach to this complex task. Novice and experienced clinicians need to understand and use these important principles to be successful in working with the wide range of clients they encounter in practice.

RECOMMENDED READINGS

Alliance of Psychoanalytic Organizations. (2006). *Psychodynamic diagnostic manual.* (2006). Silver Spring, MD: Author.

This contemporary text is steeped with important research into the validity of the interactive aspects of the clinical relationship.

Cozolino, L. (2002). *The neuroscience of psychotherapy.* New York: Norton.

Cozolino, L. (2006). *The neuroscience of human relationships.* New York: Norton.

These Cozolino texts have tremendous implications for the importance of neuroscience in understanding the relational aspects of the therapeutic encounter.

Tansey, M. J., & Burke, W. F. (1989). *Understanding countertransference: From projective identification to empathy.* Mahwah, NJ: Analytic Press.

This is the definitive text on the historical development of countertransference theory and technique.

Wallin, David J. (2007). *Attachment in psychotherapy.* New York: Guilford Press.

Wallin's work on the clinical relationship is new, profound, and highly researched.

Yalom, Irving D. (1989). *Loves executioner.* New York: Basic Books.

Many consider this excellent book the definitive narrative of the clinician's personal experience in psychotherapy. It is a must-read for anyone working in clinical practice.

OTHER RESOURCES

Bender, L. (Producer), & Van Sant, G. (Director). (1997). *Good Will Hunting* [Motion picture]. United States: Castle Rock Entertainment.

> This film is one of the strongest depictions of the importance of the therapeutic relationship and the mutual contributions of the therapist and client to that process.

In treatment. (2008). New York: HBO.

> For the reasons mentioned in previous chapters and the subtle nuances in the therapeutic exchanges between patient and therapist and the ways they further the process of treatment, this show is essential viewing for students and experienced clinicians alike.

Cultural Competence, Biases, and Blind Spots

The contemporary clinical literature is replete with material on understanding and using cultural competence in therapeutic work (Rothman, 2008; Weaver, 2005). Obviously, skilled clinicians must be aware of the wide range of client diversity in their practice, as well as how to effectively engage, assess, and work with diverse clients to bring about helpful outcomes. Many texts on diversity devote their content to describing the wide range of diverse populations to help clinicians understand the specific client groups they may encounter in practice. This can indeed be helpful, but it can often inadvertently reduce clients to a narrow and limited range of descriptors and stereotypes that may actually blind clinicians as they attempt to work with clients.

It has been my experience that the development of a culturally competent approach to clinical practice takes time, training, and—most important—experience. Enrolling in a few courses on diverse populations or cross-cultural practice does not make a clinician an expert in that area. Culturally competent clinical practice develops through the successful incorporation of the entire repertoire of clinical knowledge and skills so essential for working with clients from all backgrounds.

DEFINITION OF CULTURAL COMPETENCE

Juliet Rothman (2008), in her book *Cultural Competence in Process and Practice: Building Bridges*, sums it up quite nicely in her introduction:

> Cultural competence and sensitive ... practice are not goals to be strived for, attained, and filed away for use as needed. Rather, cultural competence is a special worldview, a way of considering self and other in the context of the whole range of human experience. Cultural competence is a lifelong process, and as we grow and mature both as professionals and private individuals,

the depth and breadth of our cultural competence is continually evolving. As we take in new experiences, process life events, understand others, experience history, and develop relationships, each one of these elements adds a piece to our cultural competence. We can never know too much about cultures and differences among peoples. It is the *journey*, and not the *destination*, that we must understand and upon which we must consciously embark. We take with us the tools and worldview of our own experience, and we use those to understand the experiences of others. (p. 3)

Rothman's quote easily transfers to the clinical relationship. The development of cultural competence in the therapeutic encounter is not a recipe book of stereotypical traits or specific techniques. To work successfully with all populations, clinicians need to develop the capacity for ongoing awareness and self-scrutiny.

Rothman's worldview is analogous to life experience as it shapes identity both within and outside of the clinical setting. Although this principle is an obvious one for competent clinical work in general, it holds even greater importance in working with the wide range of diverse clients seen in practice. Most simply, the more thoughtful experience one has with a diverse world, the more capable one is in both life and practice. Each new client experience is an opportunity for both parties to grow.

There is not general consensus on the definition of cultural competence (Weaver, 2005). The primary emphasis in culturally competent clinical practice is awareness of difference in at least some of the following areas: "Gender, Race (a social construct, but a prevalent one nonetheless), Ethnic Group, Nationality, Skin Color, Language, Religion, Ability/Disability, Sexual Orientation, Age, Social Class, Immigration Status, Region of Country, and Size and Appearance" (Rothman, 2008; p. 8).

Even this list may not capture the entire range of diversity in the area of cultural competence. The entire clinical experience is fraught with challenges related to understanding, empathy, assessment, and effective therapeutic work. The primary basis of therapeutic exchange is verbal, but the factors mentioned earlier subtly influence that verbal communication, as do the nonverbal ways in which they modulate communication.

This is not to minimize the powerful effects of prejudice, racism, and other harmful oppressive dynamics that have endured for so many centuries. It is a simple reminder that there is the potential for distortion in all human interactions. Competent therapeutic training should enable clinicians to develop the ability to negotiate the slippery slope of inevitable interpersonal confusion and challenge.

CULTURAL COMPETENCE, BIASES, BLIND SPOTS, AND WORKING MODELS OF SELF AND OTHER

One of the most effective ways to manage challenges and threats to the therapeutic relationship is through the ongoing use of the relational working models of self and client. The use of the word *relational* implies that distortions in the therapeutic process are ongoing, mutual, and cocreated. However, there are some emotional and cognitive reactions that come predominantly from the client and some that come predominantly from the therapist. Some examples will help illustrate this principle.

Case Examples: Gender

Mrs. A comes to individual therapy to work on difficulties she is experiencing with her husband. In the first session, she says to the therapist, "Well, you're a man, so you obviously don't do any housework, cooking, or cleaning and can't possibly understand my world."

On the surface, it seems that this particular interactive distortion emanates predominantly from the client's biases about men and marriage. Had the therapist previously disclosed that he did not do any housework, the situation would be quite different. This interaction may trigger a relational dynamic that has several potentialities depending on how the therapist and client explore the issue. What is important here is that the therapist understands the client's bias and empathically responds to it in a way that will help her. It would also be useful for the clinician to begin to explore his own working model of self as it relates to marriage, relationships, and so on, and how that history or identity might interface with the client.

Race

A thirty-year-old African American female psychologist has been seeing a white male doctorate in social work for clinical treatment for several weeks. The issue of race had not surfaced in initial sessions, although to the therapist, it seemed to be an important lingering factor. This point was complicated by the fact that the client had informed the clinician that she was having a romantic relationship with a white psychologist similar in age to the therapist. Quite innocently, in one session, the client happened to mention that she had decided to see the therapist because he was a white male. This began a series of lengthy discussions on race, men, relationships, and so on, and it opened the door to explore what race meant to both of them. Over time, several distortions and biases from both therapist and client contributed to confusion and clarity, as the inner worlds of both parties led to a meaningful relational world. The therapist had never dated a woman from a different race. It was important for him to constantly check his own working model of self not only in terms of relationship introjects but also in terms of presuppositions regarding race.

Ethnic Group or Nationality

Shortly after the horrific 9/11 catastrophe, a Middle Eastern man in his late twenties started seeing a white male clinician in his fifties. Needless to say, the clinician was aware of feeling a tremendous amount of anger, anxiety, and depression about the recent events. He found himself unable to meet with the client without feeling suspicious of him, his family, and the possible connections with terrorists. He also found himself feeling critical of any customs or traditions that the client would discuss in sessions.

Although an obvious countertransference reaction, the therapist had a difficult time remaining objective in sessions. He knew that not all Middle Eastern people were terrorists. He also knew that his world had been shattered, and most sources agreed that the terrorists responsible were of Middle Eastern descent. Part of him felt justified in his suspicions, and part of him felt extreme guilt for not feeling able to assume the proper professional and ethical approach to treatment.

To ensure the ability to develop and use an effective therapeutic relationship with this client, the clinician needed to continually access his working models of self and other within a relational matrix. In other words, contributions from both therapist and client influence continual interactions in the therapy. This is considered a created relationship that contains contributions from both participants and the unique relationship created between them (Saari, 1986).

Another key factor is the feelings of the client, especially as they might relate to 9/11 and the obvious public prejudice arising out of the fear of that situation. Culturally competent therapists must not only be aware of their own reactions but also be able to empathically connect with the client and understand that a relationship is developing based on both of their worldviews.

Skin Color

A young biracial (African American and Caucasian) woman in her twenties comes for her first counseling appointment with a white female social worker in her forties. As the therapist begins to explore the client's presenting concerns, she innocently asks the client how her African American identity has shaped her life. The client reacts to this statement by stating that she is biracial and does not consider herself African American. The client goes on to discuss her life in terms of living in a white community with predominantly white children; white teachers; and little, if any, contact with African Americans because white parents adopted her at birth.

This error on the part of the therapist created an initial rift in the therapeutic relationship, one that would continue to influence the process. Although the therapist and client form a solid working alliance, that initial bias created a formidable impasse.

Language and Region

Language barriers often complicate the clinical interaction, especially if the client and therapist are not able to communicate with the same proficiency. There are obvious gaps in language that fail to adequately capture the intent of certain communications, especially emotions. In fact, language in general is inherently flawed because it is an attempt to use words to communicate. There are many times when language falls short or fails to capture the intentions of the speaker (Lacan, 1968).

Music, art, dance and other forms of artistic expression demonstrate that fact, which is why the expressive therapy medium is so powerful. Many clients, especially those who have been traumatized, are better able to communicate through the use of nontraditional forms of communication because of the powerful symbolism and metaphor that are not as confining as traditional spoken language.

There is another subtler issue with language, however, that is important to examine. A blue-collar white male client in his thirties was seeing a middle-class African American female therapist in her forties. The presenting concern centered on marital issues. As Valentine's Day approached, the client began to focus on this holiday in terms of his relationship with his wife. He said, "Well, you know, Valentime's Day is coming soon, and I really want to get my wife something nice this year." The client did not say "Valentine's Day"; he said "Valentime's Day." This statement immediately caused the therapist to experience the client as uneducated, and perhaps even ignorant. It was an impulsive emotional reaction and one that caused the therapist to feel a good deal of guilt for feeling that way.

This same client had a habit of misusing other words, as well. He would often say things like, "Well, I went acrossed the street to get some lunch." The therapist found that it was not unusual for many clients from this area to use language of this nature. It appeared to be cultural, and yet misinformed.

The point is that the client's language created a biased impression in the mind of the therapist that potentially could contribute to distortions, lack of empathy, and misinterpretation of the client's intelligence. The therapist never corrected the client because she believed it was unnecessary and might also cause unneeded embarrassment. She did, however, need to continually bear in mind her own bias about language and communication to work successfully with the client. Failure to use introspection in this situation has obvious implications for the type of ongoing empathic interactions that might occur in the therapeutic relationship.

Religion and Spirituality

Religious views and spirituality are an integral aspect of many clients' lives. People come from various religious backgrounds and certainly vary in the extent to which they both practice and adhere to religious beliefs. Moreover, there is tremendous diversity of opinion within each religion. For example, many Catholics are pro-choice in their views on abortion, despite the fact that the pope and main body of the Catholic Church are pro-life. As a result, both therapist and client might enter into the therapeutic relationship with a wide range of biases about religion and spirituality.

A couple in their thirties comes to see a therapist for marital therapy. They are Baptist and believe firmly in the sanctity of marriage and that divorce is not an option under any circumstances. The therapist is also Baptist but has been divorced for several years. There are several potentially problematic issues, but one immediate dilemma is whether the therapist should eventually disclose her own marital situation to this client. How will the couple react to this fact? Will the information derail, interfere, or terminate the therapy? Is there a possibility that this information and context present an opportunity for exploration and growth in the marital therapy?

How does the couple's strong viewpoint on marriage and divorce affect the therapist? Can she remain neutral and objective given her life situation? If the therapist does not self disclose her divorce, how will the lingering effects of the working model of the couple affect her? If she continues to examine her own working model of self in relationship to her divorce, she will undoubtedly be challenged to reexamine her situation and choice.

Ability or Disability

Clients or therapists with disabilities have the potential to generate a wide range of perceptions, thoughts, emotions, prejudice, and biases for both parties, ranging from guilt and anxiety to fear. It is important for the therapist not to judge the client on the basis of stereotypes or preconceived notions of any condition. More important, as with any type of difference, the therapist must remember that each client will develop his or her unique way to incorporate, adapt, and manage their lives.

Mr. D came in for therapy to work on adjusting to his life after a debilitating stroke. Mr. D had mobility restored, and his cognitive abilities were intact. However, Mr. D continued to struggle with slurred speech and an inability to pronounce words in general and quickly. This was extremely frustrating for him, and it tended to lead him to become angry in most of his communications, especially with his wife. On the encouragement of his wife, Mr. D was seeking therapy to help improve his marital relationship.

The therapist, a white female psychologist in her early thirties, had never worked with someone who had experienced a stroke. When she began to work with Mr. D and his speech difficulties, she naively assumed that he was cognitively impaired. She began to interact with him as if he were a small child, using language that would be demeaning to an adult. She also tried to complete Mr. D's sentences because she was impatient with the time it took him to talk to her.

This type of interaction infuriated Mr. D even more than his communication with his wife. He left treatment after only a few sessions.

One might believe that the major difficulty in this vignette is the therapist's lack of knowledge about stroke victims. It is probably true that the therapist would have been more understanding of Mr. D had she been better informed. In addition, however, paying very close attention to the emotional cues from Mr. D, as well as exploring her working model of self was essential. For example, what is the nature of her frustration, and how do both she and Mr. D contribute to it? Insights from that introspection could have shed important light on Mr. D's marital dynamics, which were perhaps being reenacted in therapy.

Sexual Orientation

A sixteen-year-old adolescent male was seeing a heterosexual male clinician in his late twenties for therapy. The presenting concerns centered on the teenager's difficulty adjusting to his parents' recent divorce. The adolescent was an attractive and athletic young man who was actively involved in high school sports.

Several weeks into the therapy, the clinician found himself experiencing a strong physical attraction to the adolescent. The feelings were quite intense and extremely unusual because, to the best of his knowledge, the clinician could never remember experiencing this type of reaction to a male. The reaction was also puzzling because, from the client's account, he was heterosexual and involved with young women in his life.

The therapist silently accepted these internal reactions and never shared them with the client. He did spend considerable time exploring them in his own therapy and in ongoing consultation. The therapist speculated about this phenomenon on several levels: perhaps the client was projecting his own homosexual feelings on the therapist, perhaps the therapist had latent homosexual feelings that the client brought out, perhaps the sexual feelings were symbolic of other feelings not particularly related to physical attraction, and many other possibilities.

The therapist never arrived at any definitive explanation for these reactions and never experienced them again with any other male client. To the best of the clinician's knowledge, this client was heterosexual in his physical and romantic relationships. This experience has perplexed the clinician throughout his career. Exploring relational working models of self and other did not yield any insight. The physical reactions did not seem to interfere with the adolescent's therapy. Yet this experience meant something, sexual or otherwise, for the client and/or therapist.

This case example also illustrates that the therapy encounter generates a wide range of emotional experiences for both the therapist and the client. Not all of these are completely understood or resolved. However, this case demonstrates the importance of paying careful attention to all cognitive and emotional reactions.

A white male in his thirties came to therapy with a white male therapist in his early forties. The client was feeling isolated at work and having difficulty pinpointing the source or cause of the problem. The client was the supervisor for about ten workers in a psychiatric hospital. He liked the people he worked with but felt awkward spending any social time with them. He tended to keep to himself even though he was lonely and longed for personal companionship. This complex issue filled most of the early sessions in therapy.

The clinician gently helped the client explore the nature of his concerns and validated the client's need to be alone. This empathic attunement helped the client trust the therapist. The client gradually began to share some troubling feelings.

The client wondered whether he was gay. He wasn't sure about this because he did not see himself as the type of gay person he saw in the media. In fact, one day in session, he said, "I was watching this gay guy on TV this morning and I remember thinking what a fag, while at the same time thinking wait a minute, I'm a fag." This troubling situation helped the client and the therapist realize how different gay people can be. It also helped them both realize how different all people can be.

The power of that experience affected both the therapist and the client. It helped the client realize that defining his gay identity would be a process unique to him. The therapist recognized that his own internal working model of self would be modified to allow for the important fact that individual differences are the norm in any diverse client situation. The therapist and client grew together as the client explored his life with greater insight and sensitivity.

Age

A marital couple in their seventies came to see a male therapist in his mid-thirties for couples' work. The therapist imagined that the couple would most likely be focusing on issues related to retirement, financial difficulties, problems with their adult children or grandchildren, and so on. To his great surprise and shock, the couple focused exclusively on their sexual relationship. The wife was upset because her husband insisted that she wear sexy lingerie and perform oral sex. She was open to these activities but felt her husband was too pushy and aggressive in his approach to physical intimacy with her. The husband felt that his wife was uncooperative and should behave like a "normal wife."

The therapist did not express his feelings outwardly, but internally he was shocked. He had never thought of seventy-year-old people having sex. In his worldview, sex was only for young people, maybe up to fifty years old. Imagining sex at seventy was even disgusting to him. This important insight drastically modified the clinician's worldview and, more important, his own working model of self. Never again did he presume to know the nature of older adults' lives.

Size and Appearance

A young woman in her late twenties started therapy with a female clinician of her same age. The client was obese, perhaps 150 pounds overweight. The therapist was not overweight. The client wanted to work on developing friendships. She lived alone, worked in a job in which she had little social contact, and all of her family members were deceased. She also wanted to try to lose some weight, because she felt it might be a factor in her situation.

As the therapist began to explore the client's situation, she realized that the client used food to self-soothe. The client tended to eat when she was lonely. Eating helped her feel safe, but later she would feel guilty and disgusted with herself for eating. The client also felt that her size interfered in her ability to make friendships, which in turn made her feel lonely, which led to further eating. The therapist realized that this was an addictive cycle. Together, the client and therapist agreed to work on these issues.

As the therapy progressed, the clinician found herself feeling disgusted by the client. She did not look forward to sessions, and she began feeling less and less empathy for the client's feelings and situation. In fact, the therapist began to silently blame the client for her plight. The clinician knew this was wrong but felt compelled by the disgusting thoughts and feelings.

The therapist worked diligently to examine the ways the relational working models of self and other contributed to this impasse. Over time, two important themes emerged. First, the therapist realized that, by the client's account, virtually everyone in her life was disgusted by her. This theme of disgust also had origins in the client's early history. Second, the therapist recognized that weight was an extremely sensitive issue in the therapist's own life. She had some slight weight problems and had experienced hurtful feelings from ongoing interactions with family and friends around this issue.

Once the clinician silently identified this complex relational dynamic, she could help the client recognize the deeply personal and relational aspect of the dynamics. This insight led to significant progress in the therapy over time. Specifically, the therapist and client were able to unite in their work toward helping the client lose weight and change her perception of self.

BASIS OF PRACTICE

Cultural competence and diversity are relatively recent issues in clinical practice. Most of the early developmental and psychological theorists were white middle-aged men. Male viewpoints and thinking dominated the culture of the time. This created a huge blind spot in clinical practice. The first notable departure was the recognition that men and women were different and perhaps could be understood differently in terms of developmental and clinical theory (Gilligan, 1982). The feminist and civil rights movements modified and emphasized the important of attention to differences, clinical practice included.

From a basis-of-practice standpoint, intuition first became evident with the movements mentioned earlier. Practice wisdom evolved shortly thereafter as clinicians of different gender, race, ethnicity, and so on began to encounter experiences such as those mentioned in the short case examples in this chapter.

Most texts on cultural competence recognize that the concept is not yet fully defined or accepted (Rothman, 2008; Weaver, 2005). In that respect, the theoretical basis of practice is still in formation. However, there is some exploratory empirical evidence that will help direct practice in the future (Baldwin, Wampold, & Imel, 2007). The complexity of the issue combined with the almost-unlimited variety of diverse populations make the task daunting. Perhaps what is needed instead is an approach to empathic attunement and relational understanding similar to what this chapter has proposed.

SUMMARY

This chapter has explored the complex nature of diversity as it relates to clinical practice and the understanding and management of the therapeutic relationship. Biases and blind spots emphasize the myriad overt and subtle ways in which inevitable distortions enter the therapeutic encounter. In fact, to be culturally competent means acknowledging the ongoing difficulties in understanding differences. The use of the relational working models of self and other can be an instrumental vehicle for the clinician to navigate this important ground.

RECOMMENDED READINGS

Baldwin, S. A., Wampold, B. E., & Imel, Z. E. (2007). Untangling the alliance-outcome correlation: Exploring the relative importance of therapist and patient variability in the alliance. *Journal of Consulting and Clinical Psychology, 75,* 842–852.

   Although not specifically focused on diversity, this research article sheds important light on the client-therapist alliance.

Stampley, C., & Slaght, E. (2004). Cultural competence as a clinical obstacle. *Smith College Studies in Social Work, 74,* 333–347.

   This social work article from Smith College addresses important aspects of cultural competence in the clinical relationship.

Rothman, J. C. (2008). *Cultural competence in process and practice.* Boston: Allyn and Bacon/Pearson.

Weaver, H. N. (2005). *Explorations in cultural competence.* Tampa, FL: Thomson.

   These are two excellent texts to help beginning and advanced therapists understand and develop cultural competence.

Tansey, M. J., & Burke, W. F. (1989). *Understanding countertransference: From projective identification to empathy.* Mahwah, NJ: Analytic Press.

   A review of the Tansey and Burke text is essential for understanding the concepts and technique so important for developing culturally competent practice.

OTHER RESOURCES

Haggis, P., Cheadle, D., Yari, B., & Shulman, C. (Producers), & Haggis, P. (Director). (2004). *Crash* [Motion picture]. United States: Yari Film Group.

   This film won an Academy Award in 2005, and it is a wonderful depiction of the complexities of diversity and the human condition. Although the film does not focus on therapy, the implications for empathic understanding and intervention are obvious.

http://www11.georgetown.edu/research/gucchd/nccc/index.html

   The Web site of the National Center for Cultural Competence provides useful information on a wide range of topics related to cultural competence.

Closure, Transitions, and Endings

LOSS AND LIFE

Any therapeutic relationship eventually involves loss. In fact, clinicians should begin to plan for closure or termination from the very first session. Ironically, therapy is about coming to an ending. Clients come to treatment to resolve problems or symptoms in their lives. Forming some sort of relationship with a therapist is essential in helping them work through the presenting concerns. However, that working through also involves a loss of the therapeutic relationship. It is crucial to examine the emotional factors that affect the clinical relationship in the ending phase of treatment.

Attachment is an integral part of the human condition. To develop the ability to interact with another person in healthy and meaningful ways, infants must first be attuned by an empathic caretaker (Ainsworth, Blehar, Waters, & Wall, 1978; Bowlby, 1969; Mahler, Pine, & Bergman, 1975; Winnicott, 1965).

Human beings eventually must learn to emotionally separate from those same caretakers to a relative extent to develop their own identity and ability to function autonomously in life (Bowlby, 1973; Erikson, 1950). This type of loss is potentially painful but also is a means toward an end. The mechanism by which a person manages loss has a tremendous impact on that person's ability to function in life (Bowlby, 1980). Even Freud's (1960) classic statement emphasizes that "ego is a precipitate of abandoned object-cathexes and that it contains the history of those object-choices" (p. 19). In other words, we are who we have become emotionally invested in or attached to in life. Furthermore, the inevitable loss that occurs in such relationships through normal developmental shifts, or even death, continues to live on in us through internalization of that relationship (e.g., thoughts, memories, emotions, physical experiences). Loss and grief are a normal part of life.

The advent of neuroscience has been helpful in emphasizing the importance of attachment and loss in the development of the brain. Successful attunement enables infants to develop secure cognitive, emotional, and physical neural networks, which lead to the ability to self-soothe. In times of stress, challenge, or brief periods of separation, these internal networks are the mechanisms by which infants and small children are able to evoke a safe and secure image of caretaking that temporarily substitutes for the caretaker (Cozolino, 2002; Stern, 1985; Wallin, 2007; Winnicott, 1965).

That process, starting in infancy, becomes the basis on which all human beings are able to manage loss in life. Even abusive relationships, though unwanted, provide a type of reliable consistency. Sometimes people prefer that familiarity to separation and abandonment, something much more frightening and uncertain.

Loss, endings, and transitions are a continual process of life. Young children leave their parents to go to day care, preschool, and kindergarten. Many parents know the anxiety that accompanies watching their child get on a school bus for the very first time. That physical and emotional adjustment involves loss on the part of both children and caretakers. Yet, if done well, it benefits both parties.

In elementary school, most children are with a new teacher each academic year. In many cases, children bond with their teachers, much like primary caretakers, only to have to separate at the end of the year, never to have them as teachers again. This is an attachment, separation, and loss that usually happen every year. Each successive process of attachment and loss is hopefully a growth-promoting experience for both student and teacher.

Many children have been told about Santa Claus, the Easter Bunny, the Three Kings, and so on. Once that bubble has been burst, they feel a loss. However, the memories of those important figures remain throughout life. The ability of human beings to negotiate this process is what helps them adapt and grow. When more severe or traumatic losses occur, such as the death of a pet, friend, grandparent, sibling, or parent—or for parents, the death of a child—the process of attachment and loss is the key to emotional survival.

Adult development is also replete with attachments, separations, and loss. When a young adult leaves home, the process involves loss for both the parent and the young person. Whether it is going away to college, getting married, or moving into a first apartment, the process of separation and loss is the same. Life is filled with such complex scenarios, and so is the clinical process.

THE CLINICAL PROCESS

There have been few books written exclusively on the termination process in clinical practice. Most texts devote a final chapter to this important process. Loss and ending can be a difficult part of the therapeutic work. The termination process is often avoided in the actual clinical situation. It is not surprising that the literature is sparse or nearly nonexistent on this important topic.

It might be much more helpful if closure in the clinical process was dealt with as one of the first issues of treatment. Preparing clinicians to anticipate and plan for the transition to end treatment can lead to effective clinical work. Understanding exactly what therapy will look like at the end of treatment helps the client and therapist work toward that goal, whether the treatment is short or long term.

Joseph Walsh's (2007) *Endings in Clinical Practice: Effective Closure in Diverse Settings* is an excellent source that comprehensively examines the process of closure in the therapeutic relationship. Walsh not only examines the nature and importance of endings in clinical practice but also comprehensively explores that process through countless case examples over a variety of clinical modalities:

> Whether or not the ending of a clinical intervention is managed well can make the difference between successful and unsuccessful outcomes for the client *and* for the professional. Closure (a concept I alluded to earlier) is a process in which practitioners and clients bring their work to a mutually understood (not necessarily satisfactory) end, review their work together (successes and failures), perhaps acknowledge feelings about the relationship, and acquire an enhanced willingness to invest in future relationships. (p. 5)

The beginning of almost all therapeutic relationships starts with a question aimed at moving toward closure: "What has brought you to therapy?" This question, delivered in a variety of ways, means basically the same thing: what needs to happen for this process to end? The client may not experience the question that way, and the therapist may not be thinking about endings either, but all therapy is geared toward just that goal—an effective end.

MANAGING THE EMOTIONS OF CLOSURE

The clinical literature demonstrates that the most important variable for successful therapeutic treatment is the therapist-client relationship (Barber, 2000; Prochaska & Norcross, 2003). For a successful therapeutic relationship to develop, the client and therapist must be able to form an empathically attuned and trusting relationship. The process of developing that relationship is filled with complex emotional interactions on the part of both the therapist and the client.

The intensity, length, and nature of the clinical work itself vary greatly depending on the unique client-therapist pairing. However, for trust to develop, as in early attachments, there needs to be a degree of emotional investment in the relationship, regardless of the time frame. The creation of a unique working relationship is a special process that both participants coauthor. This process can be a deeply emotional one in short- or long-term treatment.

Much like the significant relationship among caretakers and children, siblings, friends, spouses, colleagues, and significant others, there is an emotional core that both parties experience. The therapy relationship is no different. Emotional investment of some degree is essential for the therapy to be successful.

Clients come to care for and depend on their therapists. Therapists feel a degree of responsibility and concern for their clients. There is a mutual degree of this caring and investment in all clinical relationships. The work could not happen if that caring did not exist (Barber, 2000). Over time, this investment intensifies, as do the feelings. The clinical relationship contains a degree of intimacy that forms a bond between the client and the therapist. The therapeutic encounter can contain both positive and negative experiences and feelings about both participants. These complicated emotions become part of the therapeutic work and are a vehicle through which the client and therapist can come to know each other better. Ultimately, however, the relationship comes to an end.

Therapeutic endings can be varied and filled with myriad emotional reactions on the part of both therapist and client. The recognition of those emotions is especially essential for the therapist in helping the client come to a constructive closure in the clinical work. The therapist may feel relieved that the client is ending. This relief may be justified, but it can lead to feelings of guilt and ambivalence. The therapist may feel sad to lose someone with whom he or she has spent many hours in deep, meaningful, and constructive conversation. Finding an appropriate clinical ending can be a daunting task in the best of clinical work.

Clients can become extremely dependent on the therapist. In many clinical circumstances, this is even essential for effective therapeutic work. Walking that delicate tight rope is a common occurrence in many therapeutic relationships, and it is not surprising, as attachment is so much a part of even the briefest therapeutic relationships.

Case Example: Frank

Frank, a young man in his early twenties, was in therapy for several years with a female social worker about five years his senior. Frank had just begun a career as a youth worker in a community-based agency that provided comprehensive services to adolescents and their families. Several months into his first professional position, Frank began to experience various intense feelings in his work with this population. He used the agency's consulting psychiatrist to explore some of the emotional reactions as they related to his cases. Over time, however, he began to recognize that he needed to spend more time delving deeper into his feelings than consultation would allow. Several of his colleagues were in therapy for similar reasons, so Frank sought out a referral from the agency's psychiatric consultant.

Frank's therapy spanned several years and allowed him to explore emotional issues and conflicts that were initially stimulated by his clinical work with both adolescents and their caretakers. By taking time to examine the nature of these emotional reactions, Frank was able to begin developing a working model of self that he could begin to access in his therapeutic relationships. This involved exploring his childhood, adolescence, and even young adulthood.

Frank came from a family system of alcoholism. He was the oldest of seven children and assumed various roles in his family. He was the emotional caretaker of his mother and the scapegoat for his alcoholic father. This complex and ambivalent relationship with his parents created a sense of self that was at times extremely fragile and vulnerable and at other times confident and secure. Frank learned through his therapy that taking care of others was a role that he was born and raised to do in life. He also learned that his insecure sense of self came from the physical and emotional abuse he suffered at the hands of his alcoholic father.

This history, awareness, and insight evolved over several years in therapy and resulted from continual exploration of the ways the emotions that Frank experienced in life and with clients were directly tied to his past. These important insights enabled Frank to be a more effective therapist. He became more adept in using the working models of self and other so crucial in helpful clinical work. The key to that ability was his relationship with his therapist.

Frank became very attached to his therapist. Her consistent empathic attunement and reliability helped mend the inconsistency Frank had experienced his entire childhood. He re-created and relived his early relationship with his mother in the context of the therapeutic relationship with his social worker. Although Frank recognized that his intense feelings toward his therapist were in many ways a distortion and projection from his past, he also knew there was a reality to them.

Frank tested his therapist's consistency in many ways. He needed to do this to experience a reliability that he could depend on, unlike the experience of his childhood. He also needed to feel special and appreciated to validate his childhood experiences. Frank's therapist was a constant and reliable source of corrective emotional experience for him in the years he was in therapy.

Unbeknownst to Frank, his therapist had just undergone and recovered from surgery for skin cancer shortly before he started seeing her. She had a slight scar on her face from the surgery and felt very self conscious about it. Frank did not notice his therapist's scar and often complimented her on how pretty she was. Although probably a distortion of sorts, this dynamic in the therapeutic relationship helped Frank's therapist feel better and understandably connected to Frank. Perhaps this serendipitous experience served as a crucial therapeutic mechanism for both Frank and his therapist. At any rate, Frank and his therapist felt very connected to each other and did good work together for several years.

Frank felt so comfortable with his therapist that he secretly thought he would never leave therapy. He knew that closure was important and probably necessary for clients, but he could not see himself ever leaving his therapist. Eventually, Frank asked his therapist if he could see her for as long as he wanted. Frank's therapist was tactful and diplomatic, informing him that she would continue to see him as long as there was a need to be seen. That statement relieved Frank.

Over time, Frank realized that the need to remain in therapy was tied to his fear of rejection. Being the oldest child and a caretaker of his own mother interfered in Frank's ability to have his own dependency needs met except by taking care of others. His relationship with his therapist was different. In fact, for the first time in his life, Frank was able to truly be dependent without having to take care of the other. This insight helped Frank develop greater security and, even more important, understand the value of the therapeutic relationship with his clients.

Over time, Frank began to find his therapy boring. He also found himself feeling annoyed with his therapist. She didn't seem as interested in him, and their time together did not feel as special. Frank began to explore these feelings in therapy. He soon began to recognize that there was a need to end treatment. Frank denied these feelings for many months, but he eventually recognized that ending therapy was his next step in treatment. He saw it as part of the process.

Frank eventually ended therapy. He spent many months reviewing the work he had accomplished with his therapist. He even set an ending date with her that allowed for several months to process the closure. That process and the control Frank experienced over it was perhaps the most important part of his therapy. He had not been able to experience that kind of a relationship in his life. The therapeutic encounter truly shaped and helped him grow unlike any other.

Frank no longer sees his therapist. For several years he would come for a session or two a year to touch base or rework some issue in his life. This process dwindled, though, as Frank no longer felt the need to connect with his social worker.

DISCUSSION

What is the point of this case example? Not many therapeutic relationships are so extensive, long term, or emotionally intense. The realities of insurance companies dictating twenty-session limits per year with a large deductible, or even as few as six to ten sessions per year depending on the diagnosis, is becoming more common. Closure must be adapted to the limitations of the client-therapist arrangement. Regardless of those limitations, however, closure is still an important phenomenon that is essential to the clinical process. The ending in Frank's case illustrates the importance of managing closure effectively with all clients.

This case is about attachment, attunement, consistency, caring, and reliability. Many therapeutic cases focus on similar issues. Some cases are short term; others are much longer in duration. The key to success, however, resides in the ability to develop an effective therapeutic relationship that can accomplish the goals that the therapist and client develop. Success also depends on the manner in which they manage closure.

Had Frank's therapist prematurely ended treatment, would he have survived? Yes. More important is that Frank's therapist was insightful enough to allow him to end at his own pace. In hindsight, the issue of separation, closure, and endings was at the heart of Frank's life issues.

This case illustrates how crucial it is to understand and manage the therapeutic relationship, especially when it comes to ending. Frank's experience not only helped him personally but also enabled him to become a better therapist. Paying close attention to all facets of the clinical relationship is crucial for effective therapeutic work. Handling closure effectively is important and challenging no matter how long the treatment or what the modality or theoretical approach.

SIGNALS, SIGNS, AND INDICATIONS OF CLOSURE

The therapeutic relationship is filled with myriad complex, confusing, and at times conflicting emotions. One of the most important and difficult jobs of the clinician is to try to understand and decipher the possible meanings of those emotions to help the client. As treatment draws toward possible closure, there are often emotional signals in the therapy relationship that indicate that the ending phase is near.

When therapists or clients feel boredom in a treatment relationship that has previously felt quite emotionally connected, it could be a signal that the work is drawing to a close. Often in such circumstances, the clinician realizes that the same material is covered again and again in sessions. That type of feeling may indicate that the present work of the clinical relationship is over.

Experiencing boredom in the clinical relationship in general is not necessarily a definitive indication of moving toward closure. All feelings and emotions that are experienced in the therapeutic relationship are constructed and can carry multiple meanings. A well-trained clinician will be able to use the relational working models of self and other to examine all emotions to ascertain possible meanings for the clinical encounter and intervene accordingly.

For the purposes of closure work, however, a preponderance of feelings of boredom and repetitive themes may be a signal that ending is near. Therapists and clients may find themselves compelled to fill the session with comments and interventions that do not seem to do more than kill time. This theme almost becomes the elephant in the room that begs the question, "What next?"

The client and therapist in such types of circumstances might benefit from beginning to explore the meanings of these feelings and themes in the therapy. A careful and benign examination of this process begins to clarify whether in fact the client is ready to end therapy or whether perhaps the therapy has reached a new level.

It is never safe to assume that a clinical insight is accurate. The clinician must always tactfully explore and confirm it with the client. For example, a question such as, "I've noticed we seem to be focused on discussing work lately, but work doesn't really seem to be a problem for you any more. Is there something else going on here?" Exploring issues and themes in this manner is a safe way to help the client understand the clinical process and to determine whether closure is drawing near.

The therapy process evolves over time. Sometimes feelings like these signal a need to reevaluate the therapy contract. The resolution of one issue often leads to the uncovering of deeper themes, conflicts, or issues that are even more crucial to the client. The clinical relationship is a delicate one and should be handled with great patience and professional expertise.

GUIDELINES FOR CLOSURE

Once the therapist and client have decided that closure is in order, there are some practical and pragmatic guidelines that are helpful in the process of ending.

Any therapeutic relationship can benefit from a careful review of the clinical work. In the most general sense, were the goals met? How did that come about? What did the client learn about him- or herself and life through the therapeutic process? What skills, insights, and abilities has the client developed that will help in the future? These are all essential conversation points and goals of an effective clinical closure.

Revisiting the reasons for coming to treatment in the first place is a helpful process. By examining the therapy from beginning to end (short- or long-term treatment), clients are better able to see the process and growth that have occurred over time. It allows them to own their progress and accomplishments in treatment. They may also be able to see their own limitations. This can help when approaching similar situations and relationships in the future. Finally, some discussion of what clients can do in the future should they find themselves experiencing similar conflicts helps. That discussion reassures clients about their ability to manage their lives differently and about what has actually happened in the therapeutic relationship.

Of course, not all closures are the same. Endings with children are different from endings with adolescents. Closure with families is different from closure with couples. Endings with voluntary clients are different from endings with involuntary ones. Forced closure requires a different type of approach from that when clients are fortunate enough to come to the ending point on their own.

Perhaps the most troubling—but all too common type of closure—is the abrupt ending. The client announces that today's session is the last. The client is not interested in processing closure (for a variety of realistic and defensive reasons). Even in such situations, it is important for the therapist to attempt to review the therapy situation to help the client manage the ending.

Each therapeutic ending is different and requires an approach unique to that therapeutic relationship. Walsh's (2007) text comprehensively covers this wide area with many helpful and practical approaches with a variety of populations and situations.

THE EMOTIONS OF THE THERAPIST

Throughout this chapter there has been discussion of the emotions of the therapist and the client surrounding closure. The very nature of clinical work requires some degree of emotional investment on the part of both the client and the therapist. That investment brings with it a mixture of emotional reactions regarding all facets of treatment but especially closure.

Many therapists never feel that their clients have made the gains they would have liked them to make in therapy. That is a very common experience. In some ways, it is probably an appropriate one, because the therapist's role is to help clients function in ways that are helpful in life. We can always improve as clinicians, and clients can always function better in life. Just remember that having that expectation or emotional reaction is OK—many therapists feel it.

It is also OK to feel good about one's clinical work. The therapeutic relationship is a process, and feeling proud about a successful outcome is not only appropriate but also emotionally healthy. This is one of the main reasons clinicians practice: to help others. As time goes on in a professional career, a growing sense of competence will develop. The ending of treatment is a time to hold on to those feelings as a source of validation.

There will be closures that don't feel so good. Abrupt endings, unplanned separations, and even clinical failures are inevitable in therapeutic work. Especially in the beginning of one's professional career, it is only natural that there will be the occasional failure and regret. That is a time for therapists to examine their own work and learn from the experience. Only through honest and careful examination and introspection can the clinician grow and develop. This is part of being a professional.

BASIS OF PRACTICE

The basis of practice in relationship to closure and endings in clinical work has begun to reach the fourth research level: validated knowledge. The nature of attachment and loss has long been understood as a commonsense understanding about life. Myth, stories, history, culture, and the human condition demonstrate that fact. Practice wisdom has been developing for more than a century around understanding and managing endings as an inevitable part of the clinical process. Countless case studies document the successes and failures surrounding the ending of treatment.

The research on attachment and loss has been further validated through the recent work from neuroscience (Ainsworth et al., 1978; Alliance of Psychoanalytic Organizations, 2006; Bowlby, 1969; Cozolino, 2002). The clinical studies on closure in the therapeutic relationship have just begun but look very promising (Barber, 2000; Minnix, Reitzel, & Pepper, 2005; Shulman, 1999).

SUMMARY

Closure is a crucial and essential part of the therapeutic relationship. Yet for many years, this important aspect of clinical work has been sadly neglected. This chapter has examined endings in the context of the human condition and the ways it is demonstrated in clinical treatment.

The therapist and client will experience a variety of unique and complex emotions in the therapeutic relationship, especially around closure. It is important to be able to understand and use those aspects of clinical practice to be effective with clients and grow as a clinician.

RECOMMENDED READINGS

Pausch, R. (2008). *The last lecture.* New York: Hyperion.

Pausch's national best-seller is a compassionate and deeply moving encapsulation of his lectures about his life and pending death. It is a model for dealing with endings on all levels.

Walsh, J. (2007). *Endings in clinical practice: Effective closure in diverse settings* (2nd ed.). Chicago: Lyceum Books.

> This book is *the* definitive contemporary work on closure in clinical practice. Walsh covers a broad range of topics on clinical endings with various populations and therapeutic modalities. He also addresses the many types of closures in professional practice and adds practical suggestions for handling this important issue.

Albom, Mitch. (1997). *Tuesdays with Morrie.* New York: Doubleday.

> This now-classic book is a wonderful story about life and the power of relationship.

OTHER RESOURCES

Spielberg, S. (Producer & Director). (1982). *E.T.: The extra-terrestrial* [Motion picture]. United States: Amblin Entertainment.

> There is probably no better depiction in film of the attachment, separation, and loss process than *E.T.* Steven Spielberg truly captured the compelling emotional process of life. The mutually constructed relationship between Elliot and E.T. mirrors aspects of the clinical relationship in so many ways.

Foote, H., & Van Wagenen, S. (Producers), & Masterson, P. (Director). (1985). *The trip to bountiful* [Motion picture]. United States: Island Pictures.

> Geraldine Page's marvelous Academy Award–winning role demonstrates the importance of attachment, separation, and loss in life.

Cowan, R., & Winkler, I. (Producers), & Winkler, I. (Director). (2001). *Life as a house* [Motion picture]. United States: New Line Cinema.

> This film is a compelling story about attachment and loss between a father and his adolescent son. It is the demonstration of the relationship dynamics that can be a helpful vehicle for many clinicians.

Putting It All Together

This chapter reviews and demonstrates the major concepts put forth in this text in substantial detail through comprehensive case examples that cover engagement, diagnosis and assessment, middle-phase treatment, and closure. This process will enable the beginning and experienced clinician alike to understand the application of the important concepts of attachment and the use of the interpersonal working models of self and other in the therapeutic relationship.

CONCEPT REVIEW

Attachment Theory

Perhaps the most powerful theoretical and empirical principles regarding the importance of the therapeutic relationship come from attachment theory. Studies on attachment have demonstrated the crucial importance of a secure emotional and physical bond with a primary caretaker (Ainsworth, Blehar, Waters, & Wall, 1978; Bowlby, 1969). This primary relationship sets the tone for all future relationships and predisposes human beings to seek out others in times of stress, anxiety, vulnerability, and affiliation. The therapeutic relationship is an example of the kind of special human relationship that can help provide the necessary emotional support needed to weather difficult times in life. It is no coincidence that a professional discipline has developed that is based on these fundamental and innate principles.

Psychodynamic Theories

Several key psychodynamic theories have existed for nearly a decade that address the principles, nuances, and techniques essential to establishing and maintaining a helpful therapeutic relationship.

Object relations theory is important, particularly in terms of its furthering of Freud's theory of transference and countertransference, as well as its identifying and refining of complex concepts such as projective identification. The clinical validation model developed in the mid-nineteenth century still stands out as one of the most helpful for understanding and managing the therapeutic relationship today (Racker, 1968). Concepts such as complimentary identification (emotional reactions stemming from the client) and concordant identification (empathic responses to the client), direct (coming from the therapeutic interaction) and indirect (stimulated from sources outside of the therapy), thoughts (more easily maintained) and positions (more compelling urges to the therapist) are extremely helpful in understanding and managing the clinical relationship (Tansey & Burke, 1989).

Clinical validation further elaborates how therapists can begin to distinguish between their own emotional reactions and those of the client, as well as the relational nature of the created therapeutic encounter. The relational template mentioned in chapter 1 emphasizes that, in fact, it is quite difficult to actually determine the source of an emotional reaction because of its inherent mutuality. However, the nature of the relational template enables the therapist to more successfully navigate this complex situation (McKenzie, 1995, 1999).

Figure 1 is helpful in more fully understanding the specific elements of the relational template. This figure is used in the case discussion that follows.

Idiosyncratic Self
The idiosyncratic self comprises those cognitive, emotional, and behavioral aspects of the therapist and client that are relatively free from emotional conflict, yet are a strong part of their identity. In other words, the idiosyncratic self is who we are on the basis of our unique life experiences in their totality up to the present moment.

Conflicted Self
The conflicted self comprises those cognitive, emotional, and behavioral aspects of the therapist and client tied to conflict, trauma, distress, anxiety, depression, and other emotional difficulties. In most cases, these components form the basis of the therapeutic work for the client and are potentially problematic areas for the therapist (countertransference).

Concordant Identification
Concordant identification is empathic identification and response to the client that is relatively free from emotional conflict.

Complimentary Identification
Projective identification is a good example of complimentary identification. The therapist responds to the client's emotional conflicts. These are usually communicated in unconscious ways through nonverbal communication, vitality affects

Figure 1 The Relational Template

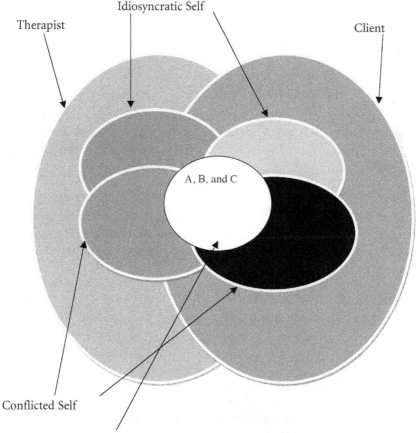

Therapist

Idiosyncratic Self

Client

A, B, and C

Conflicted Self

Relational Area of Experience: (A) Concordant and complimentary identifications; (B) thoughts and positions; (C) direct and indirect influences.

Notes: Therapist is the person providing therapy; client is the person receiving therapy. *Idiosyncratic self:* those cognitive, emotional, and behavioral aspects of therapist and client that are relatively free from emotional conflict but are a strong part of their identity. In other words, who we are is based on our unique life experiences in their totality up to the present moment. *Conflicted self:* those cognitive, emotional, and behavioral aspects of therapist and client tied to conflict, trauma, distress, anxiety, depression, and other emotional difficulties. In most cases, these components form the basis of therapeutic work for the client and are potentially problematic areas for the therapist (countertransference). *Concordant identification:* the empathic identification and response to the client that is relatively free from emotional conflict. *Complimentary identification:* Projective identification is a good example of complimentary identification. The therapist responds to the client's emotional conflicts, usually communicated unconsciously through nonverbal communication, vitality affects (movement), and tone of voice. The therapist feels compelled to respond in certain ways given the nature of the client's communication. The therapist's response typically reenacts a relational scenario from the client's life, one that has become an ongoing pattern in current relationships (Ogden, 1982; Stern, 1985). *Thoughts:* Especially in regards to complimentary identifications, therapists may feel troubled by the client's communications. However, such thoughts and emotions are not troubling enough to interfere in the therapist's approach to treatment. The therapist can silently process thoughts while engaging in the therapeutic encounter. *Positions:* The nature of the client's communications is so troubling to the therapist that he or she feels compelled to respond in ways that may not be helpful or therapeutic (e.g., arguing with the client, responding in uncaring or distant ways). *Direct influences:* interactions that come from the therapeutic relationship itself are direct influences. *Indirect influences:* Sometimes outside parties create pressure or coercion on the therapeutic relationship. Insurance companies, supervisors, parents, and even colleagues may influence and even interfere in the clinician's ability to effectively serve the client.

(movement), and tone of voice. The therapist feels compelled to respond in certain ways based on the nature of the client's communication. The response of the therapist is typically a reenactment of a relational scenario from the client's life, and one that has become an ongoing pattern in current relationships (Ogden, 1982; Stern, 1985).

Thoughts
Especially in regard to complimentary identifications, therapists may feel troubled by the client's communications. However, such thoughts and emotions are not troubling enough to interfere in the therapist's approach to treatment. Therapists are able to silently process such thoughts while engaging in the therapeutic encounter.

Positions
Positions refer to situations when the nature of the client's communications is so troubling to the therapist that he or she feels compelled to respond in ways that may not be helpful or therapeutic, such as arguing with the client or responding in uncaring or distant ways.

Direct Influences
Direct influences are those interactions that come from the therapeutic relationship itself.

Indirect Influences
Indirect influences refer to outside parties that sometimes create pressure on or coerce the therapeutic relationship. Insurance companies, supervisors, parents, and even colleagues may influence or interfere in the clinician's ability to effectively serve the client.

Self-Psychology

Self-psychology emphasizes the need for self-objects that provide emotional sustenance throughout life. Mirroring, idealizing and merging, and twinship self-objects are necessary to establish a cohesive sense of self. The therapeutic relationship is used to meet those self-object needs of most clients in one way or another. Repairing self-object deficits through an empathically attuned relationship is crucial to that process.

Relational Theory

Relational theory helps to demonstrate that most therapeutic encounters evolve out of a relational matrix that contains contributions from both therapist and client. The relational template helps the therapist determine the quality and nature of that matrix, as well as to indicate possible interventions and direction for the treatment. In many cases, through the use of the relational working models of self and other, the clinician is able to identify key emotional sources that emanate almost exclusively from the client or the therapist. In those situations, the clinical work can benefit immensely from that awareness. The process will continue to be a mutual creation of both parties, but transference and countertransference reactions do happen.

Rogerian Theory and Therapy

Carl Rogers developed theory and technique predicated on the importance of empathy in the interaction between therapist and client in the clinical relationship. He was also the first to research the role of empathy in therapeutic outcomes (Rogers, 1957). Furthermore, Rogers developed an entire theory of personality development that emphasized cognitive dissonance as one of the most powerful contributing factors to clients' emotional difficulties.

Empathic communication on the part of the counselor enables clients to carefully explore the basis of their cognitive distortions and emotions without fear of criticism. This allows clients to arrive at solutions that will enable them to function better in their world. The unique nonjudgmental quality of the therapeutic relationship and ongoing empathic responsiveness on the part of the therapist is a type of relationship not found in everyday human interactions. The mutuality inherent in family, friendship, collegial, and even work relationships does not allow for the same type of empathic healing that is the necessary basis for change in Rogerian therapy (Rogers, 1965).

Neuroscience Theory and Research

The advent of neuroscience theory and research is the glue that holds all the previous theories together. From the moment of birth and throughout life, important neural networks develop that enable humans to function in emotionally healthy ways with others. By the same token, disruption, inconsistency, trauma, and abuse can lead to major problems in neurological development that can affect all area of cognitive functioning (Cozolino, 2002, 2006; Fosha, Siegal, & Solomon, 2009).

Short- and long-term clinical approaches ranging from cognitive-behavioral therapy, psychodynamic psychotherapy, solution-focused approaches, to many types of family therapy can bring about changes in the neural networks of the brain. The unique combination of cognitive, emotional, and behavioral aspects of clinical work helps solidify new and emotionally healthier neural networks that lead to happier and healthier functioning in life.

For more than a century, the therapeutic relationship was intuitively known to help bring about change in clients' lives. However, the process could not be empirically validated. In fact, counseling and psychotherapy were believed to be more art than science. Recent advances in neuroscience research have demonstrated that clinical approaches of all kinds have the potential to change the structure of the brain and improve emotional functioning (Alliance of Psychoanalytic Organizations, 2006; Fosha, Siegal, & Solomon, 2009; Wallin, 2007).

PRACTICE TEMPLATE

In my book *Theory and Practice with Adolescents: An Applied Approach*, I discussed the clinical practice template (McKenzie, 2008). Similar to the relational working models of self and other, the clinical practice template emphasizes how all clinicians build and draw on their cognitive, emotional, and behavioral experiences in practice. The template is bare and basic when a therapist first begins to practice, but it becomes enriched and sophisticated as the therapist gains and refines clinical experience.

Experiences in practice, both positive and negative, shape each practitioner's clinical practice template. The therapist tends to rely on those approaches to practice that have been successful and quickly learns to steer away from those that are not as helpful. This process is what all clinicians experience in their professional experiences and training.

Part and parcel of this clinical practice template is the incorporation of certain theoretical models and approaches to practice. With experience, the template broadens and expands. It is not unusual for beginning therapists to cling to one or two tried-and-true clinical models. That is a natural impulse and probably good clinical judgment. However, over time, the practitioner realizes that not all clients can fit into one or two practice approaches. The relational template is fluid and dynamic. It changes with life experience and with each new clinical encounter.

Trying to fit clients into specific practice models often leads to frustration and unsuccessful treatment outcomes. As a result, clinicians begin to broaden their approach to practice to include a variety of theories and techniques. The major fundamental approaches to clinical practice tend to fall into three categories: cognitive behavioral, psychodynamic, and family systems.

Cognitive-behavioral approaches emphasize working with thoughts and behaviors. Simply put, faulty beliefs lead to unhealthy behaviors. Cognitive-behavioral therapy can be quite successful with clients whose basic difficulties can be traced to faulty assumptions and cognitive distortions (Beck, 1995). Cognitive-behavioral therapy can also be successful in short-term treatment. This approach is widely used with clients today. Clients with more complex developmental problems or severe trauma might benefit from psychodynamic approaches.

Psychodynamic approaches to practice such as object relations theory, self-psychology, relational theory, and attachment theory focus on modifying the deeper layers of self that developmental difficulties have rendered unhealthy. Attachment theory and research demonstrates the severe difficulties in human functioning that can result from traumatic or unhealthy development. Early primary relationships were not able to provide a secure-enough attachment to enable such clients to live satisfying emotional lives. The therapy relationship provides an opportunity for clients to rework these unsuccessful experiences and develop the capacity to live more satisfying lives.

Family systems approaches are aimed to help clients in their interpersonal situations as couples, groups, and families. This approach to practice examines the ways members of the system (e.g., couple, group, family) influence one another on the basis of their own needs. Cognitive, behavioral, psychodynamic, and attachment needs can figure prominently in this approach to practice. The difference is that, in family systems work, the focus is on the dynamics of the family, couple, or group, not on the individual.

One might argue that there are many other approaches to practice beyond cognitive-behavioral, psychodynamic, and family systems. That is true. However, the other major approaches to practice tend to fall into one of those three basic models.

Neuroscience theory helps explain the process by which all these approaches to practice become internalized as complex neural networks. As clinicians use any and all types of practice approaches, they begin to develop cognitive, behavioral, and affective neural networks for each. Initially, the ability to access and effectively perform certain approaches to practice takes time. Through repetition, and especially successful treatment relationships and outcomes, the clinician begins to solidify neural networks of cognition, behavior, and emotion related to specific practice theories and models (Cozolino, 2002, 2006; Fosha, Siegal, & Solomon, 2009).

Over time, these neural networks are more easily and effortlessly accessed because they have become a part of the internalized clinical practice template. The practitioner intervenes more automatically and effortlessly because the knowledge, technique, and skills have become implicit (Cozolino, 2002). Much like riding a bike, driving a car, dancing, writing, or even reading a book, there is less need to focus on the technique; it comes automatically. However, it is continually evolving on the basis of a dynamic worldview and clinical experience.

DIAGNOSTIC AND STATISTICAL MANUAL OF MENTAL DISORDERS

The most widely recognized and used diagnostic procedures to date come from the *Diagnostic and Statistical Manual of Mental Disorders,* fourth edition, text revision (DSM IV-TR) (American Psychiatric Association, 2000). The DSM IV-TR is a global standard for diagnosing clients who are experiencing emotional difficulties. Most public and private mental health agencies and facilities require their clinicians to be proficient in the use of the DSM IV-TR for diagnosing clients from their settings. All health insurance reimbursement is contingent on an approved DSM IV-TR diagnosis.

There are five axes used in a DSM IV-TR diagnosis. Axis I captures clinical disorders, or conditions that are usually the primary focus of treatment. Anxiety disorders, depression, bipolar disorder, schizophrenia, eating disorders, and substance abuse are just a few of the examples of conditions that are coded on axis I.

Axis II is for coding clients with personality disorders or who have mental retardation. If the clinician considers the personality disorder to be the primary condition, or main focus of treatment, it must be indicated on the axis II diagnosis.

Axis III is for reporting general medical conditions that are helpful in understanding the diagnoses from axis I or II. For example, a diabetic condition may contribute to certain psychological and physiological symptoms of many clients.

Axis IV is a very useful category for indicating psychosocial and environmental factors that contribute to the overall diagnostic picture. This axis is particularly useful in helping provide a broader picture of the client's life and how it may affect the understanding of the entire diagnostic picture. Economic problems, family problems, legal difficulties, and so on, all can have strong influence on the emotions of a client.

Axis V is the Global Assessment of Functioning Scale (GAF). This 0–100 scale provides clinicians with a range of descriptive types of functioning tied to numerical scoring. For example, the scale points 41–50 correspond to "serious symptoms (e.g., suicidal ideation, severe obsessional rituals, frequent shoplifting) or any serious impairment in social, occupational, or school functioning (e.g., no friends, unable to keep a job)" (APA, 2000, p. 34).

Taken together, the DSM IV-TR diagnosis is one of several useful lenses in helping clinicians diagnose and work with their client. A case example later in this chapter demonstrates the use of the DSM IV-TR diagnostic protocol and how to understand and use it contextually with the other conceptual features discussed here.

PSYCHODYNAMIC DIAGNOSTIC MANUAL

The Psychodynamic Diagnostic Manual (PDM) that has been mentioned earlier in this text is another excellent source with which to understand the client (Alliance of Psychoanalytic Organizations, 2006). Written by many of the same authors as the DSM IV-TR and based on recent attachment and neuroscience empirical research, the PDM has expanded the diagnostic realm to include several new axes. The P axis examines specific personality patterns and disorders much more broadly than does axis II of the DSM IV-TR. The M axis profiles mental functioning of the client, such as the capacity for self-regulation, internalization, and affective experience. These useful additional axes will also be discussed in relationship to the case example later in this chapter.

PRACTICE FORMULATION

In *Theory and Practice with Adolescents: An Applied Approach*, I included a modified version of Meeks and Bernet's (2001) diagnostic evaluation for assessing the adolescent client (McKenzie, 2008). A further expansion of this formulation is helpful in understanding and working with clients of all ages. I have made several additional modifications of this practice formulation for use with the case example in this chapter. The following questions can be useful in assessing and understanding ongoing work with clients in general and in developing a comprehensive biopsychosocial evaluation:

1. Is there any evidence of constitutional factors that may have contributed to the present situation? If so, how have they affected the client?
2. What level of psychosocial development do you believe the client has achieved? How have previous stages or phases influenced the present one? Do you believe the client is fixated or regressed? What factors lead you to believe that may be true?
3. What type of attachment did the client have with his or her caretakers, and how did those early developmental periods affect the client's present relationship with family, peers, and significant others?
4. Why is the client in need of service right now? Is the client self-referred, or does someone else believe he or she needs help?
5. Does the client see him- or herself as conflicted or in need of help even though he or she may not be self-referred? To what extent can they see their part in the situation?

6. Does the client have the capacity to be introspective and/or to view him- or herself objectively? What is the extent of the client's observing ego?

7. Is the client's defensive structure adaptive or maladaptive?

8. How would you assess the client's support system, and how does it affect the client's present situation?

9. Are there particular issues of diversity that heavily affect the client's situation?

10. What environmental factors are relevant to this situation?

11. What resources are available to the client in dealing with this situation? What are the client's strengths?

12. On the basis of the foregoing factors, what is your intervention plan, and what do you think the outcome might be?

The following extended case example illustrates the complex interweaving of the important concepts discussed in the text. Bear in mind that most of the principles work simultaneously and eventually implicitly as the clinician begins to develop a practice template and relational working models of self and other with every client he or she sees in practice. This may sound daunting and impossible to the novice, but eventually it becomes part of the repertoire of all practitioners.

This case example provides rich material for illustrating the concepts in action. As mentioned earlier, these concepts can be applied to various theoretical approaches and time frames. This particular case process helps demonstrate the evolution of the complex relational phenomena that are so crucial to understanding and managing the therapeutic relationship.

Case Example: Barb Revisited

The client Barb was discussed in the first few chapters of the book. Her case is revisited here at length to more fully demonstrate the concepts covered in the text and reviewed in this chapter. Barb's case is a good example of how the therapeutic relationship between the therapist and client becomes the most crucial element for successful treatment.

Background Information and Presenting Concern

Barb was a young woman in her early thirties. She was referred to a therapist in private practice from a nearby community agency. Barb was suffering from severe anxiety and looking for a therapist who specialized in working with this type of problem. The therapist was a male in his late forties who had been in private practice for more than fifteen years. He had many years of experience working with clients suffering from anxiety disorders.

Chapter 1 depicted the first counseling session with Barb. She appeared to the therapist to be extremely anxious, guarded, and defensive. The therapist recognized that he would have to move very slowly with Barb to generate enough trust to be able to get a sense of her presenting concerns.

The therapist began to initially engage with Barb by encouraging her to talk about whatever she felt comfortable discussing. Barb reacted by putting the therapist on the spot and asking him a series of questions about his expertise and ability to help her. She also continued to avoid talking at any great length about herself, what brought her to treatment, or her past.

Needless to say, this interactive style was extremely frustrating to the therapist, but it triggered him to focus on his own emotional reactions to Barb. Having little to no information about Barb, except her interactive style, the therapist began to explore his own working model of self and professional experiences with clients such as Barb. He guessed that if he was feeling frustrated, anxious, and a bit guarded and put off by the client, that perhaps she felt the same way about him, or at least about the therapeutic encounter. This helped him feel less annoyed and greater empathy and patience with Barb.

This interactive style of Barb's was also a diagnostic indicator for the therapist. In other words, he instinctively knew that there was an underlying reason Barb was so intent on maintaining her stance, even though doing so was interfering with any effective treatment. Not much could happen in the therapy as long as Barb maintained this approach. It was somewhat of a paradox or even a double bind.

From the therapist's experience, practice template, and working model of self, he realized that clients such as Barb often came from abusive backgrounds. He couldn't be sure of this, but he had enough professional experience to make a fairly educated guess about the client. If that were true, the therapist knew that only after the client felt a degree of trust and certain of her control in therapy would she begin to open up.

Barb continued to approach the first few sessions of therapy in this manner. Many clinicians would have refused to see her or become openly frustrated. The therapist patiently allowed Barb to develop a relationship at her own pace. After having barraged the therapist with myriad questions about his ability to help her, his approach to therapy, his credentials, and so on, Barb gradually began to divulge information about herself and her history.

What unfolded was an extended history of childhood sexual abuse, suicide attempts, chronic depression and anxiety, psychiatric hospitalizations, failed attempts at college education, chronic unemployment, and eventual mental health disability status, all of which led to low-income housing and a life of isolation and self-medication with alcohol and illegally obtained prescription drugs. Barb's emotional difficulties resulted from these horrendous chronic life experiences. She was a survivor, but not without some devastating consequences in terms of her emotional capabilities and adaptive functioning.

Initial Assessment

Any clinical assessment is an ongoing process and is only as good as the moment in time from which it is taken. Barb's situation is no different. Barb was an exceptionally intelligent, sensitive, and talented young woman with tremendous stamina and resilience. A DSM IV-TR five-axes assessment, PDM M and P axis assessment, along with a working practice formulation will help create a snapshot in time of her identity at the beginning of treatment with the therapist.

DSM IV-TR Five-Axes Diagnostic Assessment

Axis I. For the axis I diagnosis, in the initial phase of treatment, Barb was diagnosed with the following conditions, all of which could be the primary focus of treatment at any given point in time. First is 296.33, "Major Depressive Disorder Recurrent, Severe without Psychotic Features." Barb's life circumstances have rendered her to a deep state of depression. She does not work and spends most of her time in her apartment reading; listening to music; surfing the Internet; and self-medicating with illegally obtained prescription drugs, alcohol, and marijuana. Recurring suicidal ideation plagues her, but she has sought treatment to help her move out of this extremely dangerous situation.

Second are 303.90, "Alcohol Dependence"; 304.00, "Opioid Dependence"; 304.10, "Sedative, Hypnotic, or Anxiolytic Dependence"; and 304.80, "Polysubstance Dependence." Barb's self-medication served to insulate her from the horrific events of her life. Her chronic polysubstance dependence was a major focus and complication of the treatment discussed further here.

Third is 300.23, "Social Phobia." Because of the extreme abuse and trauma Barb has suffered, she is reticent to venture out of her apartment often. She is particularly afraid of storms, which remind her of specific abuse incidents in her childhood. Barb is uncomfortable engaging in any type of prolonged conversation with anyone, despite the fact that she is very intelligent and articulate.

Fourth is 309.81, "Post-Traumatic Stress Disorder." Barb continually suffered from the recurring thoughts and emotions related to the chronic abuse and trauma she experienced throughout her childhood to the present time of her treatment with the clinician.

Fifth is 300.02, "Generalized Anxiety Disorder." Because of the severe and chronic nature of her traumatic life experiences, Barb constantly experienced overwhelming anxiety. Neuroscience theory would explain these phenomena as neurological cognitive, emotional, and experiential trauma stored in the amygdala in the lower portion of the limbic system in the brain.

Axis II. Part of Barb's axis II diagnosis is 301.83, "Borderline Personality Disorder." Barb's chronic childhood abuse and trauma, combined with erratic and inconsistent caretaking led to the development of borderline personality disorder. It is debatable whether this diagnosis should be considered primary because so many of the axis I diagnoses were also a major focus of the treatment. However, Barb's chronic feelings of emptiness, substance dependence, impulsivity, self-mutilation, and so on, were also a major area of work in the therapy.

Axis III. Barb experienced chronic health problems resulting from her polysubstance dependence. Most of these were nonspecific but significantly interfered in her day-to-day functioning.

Axis IV. Barb was chronically unemployed, on disability, had few if any friends, and was estranged from her family.

Axis V: GAF 35 at the beginning of therapy. Barb came to treatment in an especially challenging place. Barb was barely surviving both physically and emotionally. The therapy in many ways was a last resort for her.

It is important for any clinician to bear in mind that the DSM IV-TR assessment is a particularly symptom focused, atheoretical, and relatively limited process. However, it is one of many useful lenses through which to understand the client. Another helpful assessment utility is the PDM and the M and P axes, which examine mental functioning and personality patterns and disorders (Alliance of Psychoanalytic Organizations, 2006).

Psychodynamic Diagnostic Manual

M Axis of Mental Functioning. The M axis of the *PDM* "describes categories of basic mental functioning that we believe helps clinicians to capture the complexity and individuality of the patient" (Alliance of Psychoanalytic Organizations, 2006, p. 73).

The M axis categories are based on extensive contemporary research indicating that mental capacities can be measured. Within the M axis are nine specific categories that provide a rich picture of the internal experiences and capabilities of the client. Barb's case example will be examined using the M axis categories.

For the category "Capacity for Regulation, Attention, and Learning," Barb appears to be an exceptionally intelligent individual, especially as evidenced by her language, thought processes, and memory. However, in times of emotional difficulty, she is unable to concentrate, focus, process, or stay connected in even the most basic social situations. This type of difficulty is a common occurrence and almost impossible to predict.

For the category "Capacity for Relationships and Intimacy (Including Depth, Range, and Consistency)," Barb has the desire and occasional ability to form intimate relationships, but her legitimate fear and anxiety of others, based on her life experiences, consistently compromise, derail, or destroy them. This presents an enormous challenge in her everyday life and is demonstrated profoundly in the relationship with the therapist.

For "Quality of Internal Experience (Level of Confidence and Self-Regard)," Barb consistently belittles herself and does not believe she is a good person or is in any way worthwhile. She consistently discusses feeling empty and feels she has no self.

For "Affective Experience, Expression, and Communication," in the initial phase of therapy, Barb seemed unable to demonstrate much, if any, emotion. Her communication was extremely void of emotion. In fact, often she would say that she did not feel or was not sure how to describe the emotional state she was experiencing. This initial picture changed as the therapy relationship developed, but it made it very difficult and frustrating for the clinician to intervene in almost any way with the client in the beginning part of therapy.

For "Defensive Patterns and Capacities," in the initial phase of therapy and fairly consistently throughout the course of treatment, Barb was extremely cautious, guarded, and defensive in her interactions with the therapist. This usually took the form of most of the primitive types of defenses such as projection, denial, and projective identification. There were many times that the client's defenses bordered on delusional projections toward the therapist. These types of reactions made it very difficult and challenging for the clinician to maintain an empathic connection and sustained progress in the clinical work with Barb. The treatment had the sense of two steps forward and one step back, throughout its course.

For "Capacity to Form Internal Representations," the horrific childhood abuse and inconsistent caretaking Barb experienced severely compromised her internal representations of self and other, which should have developed in early infancy and continued throughout life. As a result, she did not experience a cohesive or consistent sense of self (e.g., "I am basically a good person"). Instead,

Barb fluctuated between feeling she was utterly worthless and insignificant and having a sense that she might have a few redeeming qualities, such as her intellect. The inability to internalize a soothing representation of the primary caretaker complicated Barb's ability to engage with the therapist and, more important, to hold an image of him in her mind outside of therapy. As we will see below, the clinician and client were eventually able to make some significant progress in that area through the use of transitional phenomena, but that process was tedious and fraught with derailment (Winnicott, 1965).

For "Capacity for Differentiation and Integration," because of Barb's horrific abuse and compromised developmental relationships, she felt that she did not have a self. This resulted in extreme self-medication, self-mutilation, and the consistent inability to trust others and form relationships. In the therapy situation, Barb consistently became angry and enraged with the therapist because of her fear that she could not trust him. This resulted in ongoing projections and blaming based on her view of self and others.

For "Self-Observing Capacity (Psychological-Mindedness)," Barb had the capacity to reflect on her own experience and those of others, but her persecuted sense of self continually distorted her ability to have relative objectivity, which led to problems in her everyday life and especially in the therapeutic relationship.

For "Capacity to Construct or Use Internal Standards and Ideals: Sense of Morality," the client seemed to have established a basic coherent sense of reality. However, because of her harsh and punitive past, she tended to rationalize her experiences and decisions on the basis of distorted impressions of others (e.g., she would prejudge the therapist's ideas because of her distorted fear of his impressions of her).

P Axis: Personality patterns and disorders. The DSM IV-TR presents a primarily behavioral assessment protocol for diagnosing a range of personality disorders. The PDM dramatically expands the understanding and assessment of personality disorders based on current research (Alliance of Psychoanalytic Organizations, 2006). The PDM recommends that clinicians evaluate individual clients' personality on dimensions of severity by the following capacities:

- To view self and others in complex, stable, and accurate ways (identify);
- To maintain intimate, stable, and satisfying relationships (object relations);
- To experience in self and perceive in others the full range of age-expected affects (affect tolerance);

- To regulate impulses and affects in ways that foster adaptation and satisfaction, with flexibility in using defenses or coping strategies (affect regulation);
- To function according to a consistent and mature moral sensibility (superego integration, ideal self-concept, ego ideal);
- To appreciate, if not necessarily conform to, conventional notions of what is realistic (reality testing);
- To respond to stress resourcefully and to recover from painful events without undue difficulty (ego strength and resilience). (Alliance of Psychoanalytic Organizations, 2006, p. 22)

On the basis of these basic principles, the P axis emphasizes that all personality disorders are within a fundamental range of personality organization from healthy to neurotic and finally borderline functioning. Therefore, borderline personality disorder is not listed as a separate disorder but is considered present as one of several guiding elements of all personality disorders. This is a powerful and extremely useful premise from which to explore, assess, examine, and treat the wide range and continuum of personality disorder clients. Furthermore, the PDM suggests that there is a range of functioning within all diagnosed personality disordered clients. The significance of this broader, more comprehensive, and humane categorization is that it allows for a wider range of clinical understanding and intervention.

Barb clearly exhibits many, if not all, of the DSM IV-TR criteria for borderline personality disorder. The etiology of this diagnosis is clearly beyond her control and related to her abusive and developmentally neglected life. The P axis helps expand Barb's personality disorder diagnosis in a way that can be extremely beneficial to her in the therapy.

In addition to the borderline personality disorder underpinnings inherent in the definition of the P axis, Barb seems to exhibit several other personality patterns and/or disorders. She fits the PDM diagnosis of narcissistic personality disorder (P104.2 Depressed/Depleted). The client feels a chronic sense of emptiness and seeks people to idealize while continually being disappointed in them. This is an especially challenging dilemma in the therapeutic relationship.

Barb also appears to demonstrate traits of masochistic (self-defeating) personality disorder (P106.2 relational masochistic), depressive personality disorder (P107.1 introjective), somatizing personality disorder (P108), anxious personality disorder (P111), and dissociative personality disorder (P114) (Alliance of Psychoanalytic Organizations, 2006, pp. 15–64).

The client has had difficulty maintaining relationships because of her extremely poor self-concept, feelings of worthlessness, and belief that she is unlovable. She has chronic feelings of depression related to her lifelong history of abuse that interfere in her ability to sustain enough consistent energy to manage her life beyond day-to-day living in her apartment. Her chronic physical complaints have been difficult to definitively diagnose, which may suggest somatic etiology. She is chronically anxious and exhibits dissociative-like behavior in sessions with the therapist.

All of these factors paint a picture of a complex individual who is extremely difficult to consistently engage with in empathic treatment. The case discussion helps demonstrate these challenges and how the therapist was able to help Barb in therapy.

The Practice Formulation

Before proceeding with the case example, one more assessment rubric will be examined to provide a comprehensive picture of this client. The practice formulation asks twelve key questions aimed to capture a comprehensive developmental, social, and environmental picture of any client. Meeks and Bernet (2001) developed the initial model for working with adolescents in their classic text *The Fragile Alliance*. I elaborated and expanded on the model in *Theory and Practice with Adolescents: An Applied Approach* (McKenzie, 2008). A further modification of this model is useful for understanding all clients, including Barb.

First, is there any evidence of constitutional factors that may have contributed to the present situation? If so, how have they affected the client? This question typically explores the extent to which there may be organic or neurological factors that have significantly affected the development of the client, such as attention-deficit disorder, brain abnormalities, a predisposition to depression or alcoholism in the family, and so on. In Barb's case, the therapist was not able to ascertain the extent to which constitutional factors played a part in her developmental history.

Second, what level of psychosocial development do you believe the client has achieved? How have previous stages or phases influenced the present one? Do you believe the client is fixated or regressed at all? What factors lead you to believe this may true? Barb is chronologically in Erikson's (1950) stage of intimacy versus isolation, in which the major task is that of developing significant relationships with others in which identity can flourish through the sharing of the private aspects of self. This usually happens in the context of an intimate sexual relationship with another. This client has not had the opportunity to progress to that level of psychosocial development because of the abuse and neglect she has been subjected to her entire life. This does not mean that Barb has not been involved in sexual relationships; however, they have not reached a level of intimacy consistent with Erikson's definition. By the same token, the client has been able to sustain social relationships, but they, too, have been compromised by her anxiety, suspiciousness, and fears.

The concepts of fixation and regression are typically used to delineate the developmental challenges that ensue from life circumstances. Fixation refers to the individual's being emotionally stuck in a certain level of development, unable to move much beyond that level because of circumstances that have rendered him or her tied to the developmental task of that particular phase. Regression refers to the notion that an individual has attained a degree of the developmental accomplishment but traumatic circumstances have led him or her to regress to an earlier developmental stage because of its familiarity and safety. For example, a child who has been successfully toilet trained may regress to bedwetting under times of unusual stress, trauma, or abuse.

Barb probably is both fixated and regressed in many of the developmental challenges of psychosocial life. However, her inability to successfully negotiate Erikson's (1950) phase of trust versus mistrust appears to have dramatically compromised her ability to traverse any of the subsequent ones with much success. Therefore, she is probably "stuck" in that stage, which will become the focus of much of the therapy.

Third, what type of attachment did the client have with his or her caretakers, and how did early developmental periods affect the client's relationship with family, peers, and significant others? Barb's early development appears to have been fraught with chronic abuse and neglect, resulting in a fragile, fragmented, and inconsistent sense of self and identity. As a result, she did not develop a healthy attachment in her relationships with primary caretakers. She was not able to attain a stable sense of object constancy or self-constancy. This seems to have led to the development of many of her PDM personality disorder difficulties as well as the other DSM IV-TR diagnoses.

This type of development has significantly affected the client's ability to engage in and sustain virtually any meaningful relationships in her life. Barb seems to experience people and self as alternating versions of either all good or all bad entities. Barb's approach to therapy has aimed to try to develop the understanding and ability to develop more consistent, healthy, human connections.

Fourth, why is the client in need of service right now? Is the client self-referred, or does someone else believe he or she needs help? Surprisingly, Barb is self-referred. She is quite invested in trying to establish a healthier life for herself. She lives in relative isolation. No one knows she is in therapy. Barb very much wishes to be able to feel better about herself and others.

Fifth, does the client see him- or herself as conflicted, or in need of help, despite the fact that he or she may not be self-referred? To what extent can the client see his or her part in the situation? Barb definitely sees herself as conflicted and in need of help; however, her tendency toward severe emotional distortions, based on her primitive defenses, such as projections, denial, splitting, and so on (conflicted self), often compromise her cognitive and emotional ability to recognize her contribution to her situation.

Sixth, does the client have the capacity to be introspective and/or able to view him- or herself objectively? What is the extent of the client's observing ego? Barb appears to have the ability to be introspective, but primitive defensive structure and fragmented personality continuously distort that ability. It becomes difficult for her to see herself as others might, given her anxious fluctuation in mood and sense of self. In other words, Barb's negative identity interferes in her capacity for objectivity. The therapy relationship offers her an opportunity that she does not have in her life outside of counseling. The therapist is dedicated to understanding her without any expectations for mutuality, which could confuse and put undue pressure on the client. A newly created relationship with the therapist can help provide attachment neural networks that can begin to alter Barb's sense of self and ultimately her relationships with others.

Seventh, is the client's defensive structure adaptive or maladaptive? As discussed earlier, Barb's defensive structure is primarily of a primitive nature based on her compromised development and chronic abuse. She occasionally uses more mature defenses such as rationalization, intellectualization, and reaction formation, but her primary defenses tend to be projection, denial, splitting, and projective identification.

Eighth, how would you assess the client's support system, and how does it affect the client's present situation? Barb lives in virtual isolation, spending almost all of her waking time in her apartment listening to music, surfing the Web, and reading. Her support systems are the inanimate objects that serve to soothe her, along with illegal drugs and alcohol. At the beginning of treatment, she was ambivalent about establishing social contact, but over time, as the therapy relationship unfolded, she began to yearn for it.

Ninth, are there particular issues of diversity that heavily affect the client's situation? As discussed in chapter 4, cultural competence and diversity encompasses a broad range of factors that require consistent empathic responsiveness on the part of the clinician. Barb has experienced a horrendous life of abuse and neglect. This is an experience that many human beings are fortunate enough to avoid. Barb has not been so lucky. Her unique makeup and experiences require that the clinician be especially sensitive to her tendency to distort and to mistrust herself and others. This necessitates an ongoing use of the relational working models of self and other on the part of the therapist to help the client develop a new experience of self in the clinical relationship.

Tenth, what environmental factors are relevant to this situation? Eleventh, what resources are available to the client in dealing with this situation? What are the client's strengths? Barb has been on disability and unemployed for several years. She has extremely limited resources and lives on disability from paycheck to paycheck. This situation severely limits her opportunities.

However, Barb is very intellectual, well read, and has the capacity for intro-spection and insight from time to time. She is relatively young and healthy. She has survived extreme developmental neglect, trauma, and abuse for many years. Most important, Barb has voluntarily come to therapy and is highly motivated to change her life. This, above all else, seems to be her greatest strength.

Last, on the basis of the foregoing factors, what is your intervention plan, and what do you think the outcome might be? Barb seems to be in need of a therapeutic relationship that will help her repair the severe deficits that have developed from the neglect, trauma, and abuse she has suffered in life. This can be facilitated through an empathic, consistent, and reliable relationship with a therapist that can endure the emotional challenges that Barb will inevitably use to protect her fragile sense of self. Eventually, new neural networks of emotion, cognition, and behavior will develop and solidify, replacing the previous dys-functional patterns and representations of self and other. This requires constant vigilance on the part of the clinician through a consistent use of the relational working models of self and other and the practice template.

Engagement

Given the information discussed above, it stands to reason that the engagement phase of therapy with Barb was quite daunting. The therapist quickly came to realize that the client's working model of self was filled with conflict, and that this conflict caused her to interact in consistent and predictably suspicious ways. However, the therapist also needed to continually access his own working model of self to guard against thoughts and positions that might derail the treatment (see Figure 1).

From a purely countertransferential standpoint, the therapist was aware of his own childhood abuse and how the internalizations and representations of those experiences had shaped his identity. On the one hand, those personal experiences enabled the therapist to have a perspective that could help in his concordant or empathic identifications with the client. On the other hand, accessing those memories, thoughts, emotions, and even behavioral images had the potential to distort his ability to objectively perceive and respond to Barb.

This is not an unusual or even problematic situation if therapists are aware of their conflicted self. The problem lies in those situations when clinicians have not done enough of their own therapeutic work. In those cases, it is quite common for the therapist and client to continually run into distortions, misunderstandings, and disruptions in the therapy.

Barb refused to discuss any personal history in the beginning of therapy. The therapist intuitively recognized that this was an issue of control and that the client needed to feel a certain sense of trust before she would be able to share much, if anything, about herself. Although this client's circumstances are extreme, the therapeutic principles involved in managing them are not. Every therapist must find a way to establish a trusting relationship at the client's pace, regardless of the concerns, type, or length of treatment.

To begin, the therapist encouraged Barb to talk about how she was feeling or thinking that day or to simply tell him what she did that day. Although hesitant to comment even about those seemingly benign things, Barb slowly began to open up about her days, weeks, and even a sense of her feelings. Gradually, the therapist became able to piece together the history of her life that formed the basis of the assessment.

Barb found it difficult to face the therapist and engage in even casual conversation. She asked if they might play cards while they talked. The therapist recognized that this might be a helpful and nonthreatening way to engage. He also suggested that Barb journal her thoughts and emotions between sessions as a nonthreatening way to communicate. Barb was an excellent writer and actually preferred that type of communication. She engaged with the therapist more quickly through journaling than through the tediousness of face-to-face conversation in session.

Once the journaling began, it wasn't long until Barb was able to present her history to the therapist. From her perspective, the client had experienced chronic and prolonged emotional and sexual abuse from her mother since childhood. She also remembered spending a good deal of time alone when her mother would leave the home for extended periods of time. This seemed to have occurred during the client's preadolescence. Barb was one of four siblings, and her parents divorced in her early childhood. Barb lived with her mother after the divorce, and her other siblings lived with her father. Barb recalled having a distant and estranged relationship with her father throughout most of her life.

As Barb grew older, she began to experience more emotional difficulties that eventually led to a series of suicide attempts and psychiatric hospitalizations. Her mother tended to distance herself from Barb's difficulties. As a result, in early adulthood, Barb secured disability status and low-income housing, and began a solitary lifestyle. The early phase of therapy consisted of Barb telling the therapist these important tales of her life. However, like most clients who have struggled with sexual abuse, Barb could often recount the events (most often through journaling), but she had a difficult time remembering or connecting them to emotions. Even when she could feel something, it was quite difficult to put a name to the emotion (i.e., she was not sure if she was feeling anger, fear, guilt, and so on).

The beginning of therapy consisted almost exclusively of the therapist and the client finding a way to negotiate a level of trust for Barb to be able to share aspects of herself. Barb barraged the therapist with constant sarcasm and insults as she struggled to trust him. This uneven but oddly predictable interactive sequence became part of the created relationship. The therapist continually relied on his evolving relational model of self and other to maintain patience, empathy, and structure in the therapy (see Figure 1).

Middle Phase

Any attempt to delineate the specific phases of clinical treatment is doomed to failure; therapy by any definition is a work in progress. Engagement and assessment are ongoing processes that the very nature of the reciprocal interactions and contributions of both the therapist and client continually modify. That said, however, there appears to be a progression that evolves in any form of clinical treatment, be it short or long term, regardless of the modality or theoretical orientation.

At some point in effective treatment, engagement has been established insofar as the therapist and client seem comfortable enough with each other and the relationship to embark on treatment goals. Once that has happened, the therapy enters a new phase, the middle phase of treatment. It is in the middle phase that the goals of therapy are met and a move toward closure ensues.

Barb and her therapist reached the middle phase of treatment through a careful and delicately traversed series of interactions, communications, clarifications, and understandings regarding the therapeutic work. Barb began to tentatively believe in and experience the therapist as a trustworthy person in her life. This happened because the therapist patiently responded to Barb's anxiety, worries, fears, anger, and so on with empathic understanding and nonjudgmental communication. The clinician continually used the ever-evolving relational working model of self and other to examine his emotional reactions to be reasonably certain that he was not responding in ways that disrupted or derailed the therapy (see Figure 1, particularly the intersections of idiosyncratic and conflicted selves).

The client's periodic sarcasm, blame, projection, and denial were a continual source of frustration for the therapist in the middle phase of treatment. Barb often communicated this through her journals, in which she would accuse the therapist of hating her, judging her, misunderstanding her, and generally not being able to be helpful and effective in any way. The therapist responded to these communications (emotional pain) by gently and carefully exploring the origins and reasons for the thoughts and feelings. For example, Barb might write about how she used drugs to self-medicate the feelings she experienced after discussing an abusive event in the therapy session. She might then write about feeling convinced that the therapist hated her and probably didn't want to have anything to do with her.

The therapist would patiently explore the client's concerns, acknowledge his own distortions and emotions that were consistent with Barb's suspicions, and explore those areas in which they had different impressions (examination of the conflicted self of both therapist and client from the relational template in Figure 1). The clinician did not easily convince Barb, because so much of her life had been filled with abuse, deceit, lies, and trauma. Nonetheless, the therapy seemed to move ahead in a positive direction of trust over time. This happened because Barb's real experience of the therapist began to consistently reflect what he communicated to her—that he did care about her and was a safe and trustworthy person.

As Barb's trust and attachment to the therapist continued to develop, she began to share more and more of the details of her abusive past. This both relieved and annoyed her. On the one hand, it was helpful to have someone to share these painful experiences with and to feel a justified sense of validation. On the other hand, reliving the experiences intensified the client's anxiety, depression, and posttraumatic stress reactions.

Barb's polysubstance abuse and dependence began to increasingly interfere with and become a major focus of the treatment. Her traumatic psychiatric history made Barb averse to any type of inpatient treatment for either substance abuse or mental health concerns. In fact, she vowed that she would rather commit suicide than ever return to any form of inpatient hospitalization. The therapist recognized that given her history, he would have to creatively negotiate the treatment in a way that precluded psychiatric or substance abuse hospitalization.

However, the therapist also realized that to help the client with her treatment goals, he would have to carefully balance working on Barb's anxiety, depression, and trauma and the resultant substance use. Many approaches to addictions specify that underlying mental health issues cannot be dealt with until the substance addiction is treated (Doweicko, 2002).

However, other more contemporary theorists recognize that the dual-diagnostic issues are inseparable both in etiology and in treatment (Levin, 2001). The latter was the approach the clinician used with Barb.

From a neuroscience perspective, the amygdala housed much of the client's trauma. Early, chronic, pervasive abuse and trauma form dysfunctional neural networks of cognition, emotion, and behavior that become reactivated in times of stress, particularly posttraumatic stress episodes. Because of her dysfunctional and traumatic life events, Barb was not able to develop the self-soothing mechanism that usually occurs through an attuned relationship with an empathic caretaker. As a result, she developed self-destructive coping mechanisms, such as her polysubstance dependency, self-mutilation, and social isolation. Her traumatic life events also predisposed her to functioning to a much greater extent from her right brain (e.g., emotions) than her left (e.g., cognition) (Cozolino, 2002, 2006; Fosha, Siegal, & Solomon, 2009).

The irony of the middle phase of therapy for this client was that it was both a blessing and a curse. An attuned therapeutic relationship helped to begin establishing and rerouting dysfunctional neural networks through a process called neural plasticity (Cozolino, 2002). This enabled Barb to begin to feel better and restore a more positive sense of self. However, as she uncovered more and more trauma and abuse in the therapy, her primitive defense mechanisms and reactive anxiety intensified.

This resulted in greater and greater use of illegal substances, which invariably sent Barb into deeper depression and brought on emotional setbacks. For instance, Barb began to feel a desire to venture outside her apartment to volunteer and begin exploring possible employment. However, as she discussed these experiences in therapy, they reenacted traumatic memories that led to the self-destructive behaviors that kept her isolated in her apartment.

From a countertransference standpoint, the therapist felt a continual sense of guilt and responsibility for the client. He felt handcuffed by Barb's fluctuating thoughts, emotions, and behavior. Her fairly consistent drug use and self-mutilation interfered in his ability to feel certain about a particular course of treatment. As a result, the therapist found himself treating the client in the middle phase of treatment with an integrative cognitive-behavioral and psychodynamic approach to her difficulties (Prochaska & Norcross, 2003).

Careful attention to the relational template and the working models of self and other helped the therapist determine when it was appropriate to delve deeper into the client's emotional life and when it was more prudent to stay closer to the surface and stabilize her emotions through appropriately timed cognitive and behavioral interventions. For example, when Barb began using illegal substances more for self-soothing in response to a posttraumatic stimulus, the therapist geared the sessions and conversation toward day-to-day activities and conscious thoughts about functioning in the here and now. When she seemed more stable and capable of exploring deeper emotions, the therapist would carefully resume that process.

Both psychodynamic and cognitive-behavioral work were necessary with Barb. To function in her day-to-day world, establish relationships, and resume a place in the workforce, Barb needed to gain a greater understanding of her emotions and the way they interfered in her success. In addition, the ongoing therapy relationship enabled her to develop new neural networks and a very real sense of trust and safety regarding life. When her emotions became too overwhelming, the therapist used cognitive-behavioral work to help stabilize her and minimize her affective reactions. This delicate balance was tedious but effective over time. Ultimately, Barb made significant enough improvement that the therapy entered the closure phase.

Closure

Through this careful and tedious therapeutic process, the therapist and client were able to gradually make significant progress in the clinical situation. Although the reality of the treatment was two steps forward one step back, Barb did meet many of her original goals.

She slowly ventured out of her world of isolation, first by volunteering and then securing employment that led to her getting off of disability. Barb continually struggled with drug abuse issues, especially as she experienced posttraumatic stress episodes that venturing outside her comfort zone had triggered. However, with the constant empathy and support of the therapist, the client was able to develop coping mechanisms that gradually replaced the need to self-medicate and cut herself.

The delicate and carefully timed use of an integrative approach to treatment using cognitive-behavioral and psychodynamic methods was the key to the success of this treatment. In addition, the therapist's use of the relational template and the working models of self and other were instrumental in enabling him to have clarity of focus in working with Barb.

It was only through the continual ability to sift out and understand the complicated relational matrix with Barb that the therapist could be consistently empathic and know when to shift from surface-oriented therapy to intrapsychic and affective processing.

Barb continues to do well in her life after several years of therapy. She still struggles with substance abuse and has instability in many of her social relationships. However, she does have relationships, has ventured outside of her isolation, is employed, and feels better about herself.

As mentioned in chapter 5, closure is never perfect or final. *Transition* is probably a better word for the process. This client seems to have improved and transitioned to a better life than she had before the therapy. She may need to continue to seek out treatment as she moves on with her life. What is important is that she is in a better place because of the therapy relationship that helped her establish a better sense of self.

BASIS OF PRACTICE

The concepts and their application in this chapter represent all four levels of research knowledge. For centuries, humans have intuitively understood the value and necessity of attachment and empathy in human development. Practice wisdom and case studies from Sigmund Freud's time to the present (including this chapter) demonstrate the anecdotal validity of this knowledge. The theories regarding the therapeutic relationship have been evolving since the early 1900s. The advent of attachment theory and research in the mid-1900s combined with neuroscience theory and research clearly demonstrate the importance of attachment in emotional and neurological development, as well as the need to incorporate that knowledge into approaches to practice that target the therapeutic relationship as a curative factor (Ainsworth et al., 1978; Alliance of Psychoanalytic Organizations, 2006; Bowlby, 1969, 1973, 1980; Cozolino, 2002, 2006; Fosha, Siegal, & Solomon, 2009; Tansey & Burke, 1989).

SUMMARY

There is no typical case in therapy. Any that had been chosen for this chapter would have fallen short or been incomplete in some way as an explanatory model. This case example and text, for that matter, was not designed to demonstrate comprehensive theories and techniques for practice. Other sources cover, and continue to cover, that information. However, this text emphasized the importance and essential necessity of understanding and using the therapeutic relationship as a primary vehicle for success in practice.

The relational and practice templates combined with the working models of self and other are important adjunctive pieces of the clinical repertoire for any therapist. This text has provided a sorely needed, long-overdue examination and explication of that knowledge. Hopefully this material will be of value for both beginning and experienced clinicians from all disciplines that provide clinical services regardless of time frame, theoretical paradigm, or modality.

RECOMMENDED READINGS

Alliance of Psychoanalytic Organizations. (2006). *Psychodynamic diagnostic manual.* (2006). Silver Spring, MD: Author.

> This book has also been cited and discussed throughout the text, but it is worth mentioning again what a valuable resource it is for expanded diagnosis and discussion of recent empirical research on attachment and neuroscience as it relates to practice.

Cozolino, L. (2002). *The neuroscience of psychotherapy.* New York: Norton.

Cozolino, L. (2006). *The neuroscience of human relationships.* New York: Norton.

> These important books have been mentioned and cited several times throughout the text. Cozolino does a tremendous job of not only explaining the neuroscience concepts in development but also demonstrating how they apply to the therapeutic relationship.

Fosha, D., Siegal, D. J., & Solomon, M. F. (2009). *The healing power of emotion: Affective neuroscience, development and clinical practice.* New York: Norton.

> This text is a compilation of contemporary articles on the emotional aspects of neuroscience.

Prochaska, J. O., & Norcross, J. C. (2003). *Systems of psychotherapy: A transtheoretical analysis* (5th ed.). Florence, KY: Thomson Brooks/Cole.

> Prochaska and Norcross's book is a wonderful review of the approaches to clinical work and, most important, a transtheoretical model of practice that carefully integrates clinical approaches in an informed manner.

Tansey, M. J., & Burke, W. F. (1989). *Understanding countertransference: From projective identification to empathy.* Mahwah, NJ: Analytic Press.

> Tansey and Burke's text is recommended here as a continual reminder to all clinicians to use a disciplined examination of self and other to provide effective treatment.

OTHER RESOURCES

In treatment. (2008). New York: HBO.

> This excellent series depicts the complexities of engaging in clinical treatment through the use of the therapeutic relationship. The therapist Paul (Gabriel Byrne) is not perfect but flawed and emotional; but he certainly demonstrates the hazardous reality of engaging in practice.

Bender, L. (Producer), & Van Sant, G. (Director). (1997). *Good Will Hunting* [Motion picture]. United States: Castle Rock Entertainment.

   Robin Williams gives an outstanding, Academy Award–winning performance as a vulnerable therapist who uses the therapy relationship to help a young man who had been severely abused throughout his childhood and is struggling with the damage it has caused him. The technique is not perfect, but the relationship is an authentic example of real practice.

Bodie, C. (Producer), & Mangold, J. (Director). (1999). *Girl, interrupted* [Motion picture]. United States: 3 Art Entertainment.

   This film depicts the emotional struggles of several young women in a psychiatric hospital of the 1960s. It is important both as a character study and demonstration of the power of the therapy process and relationship.

Works Cited

Ainsworth, M. D. S., Blehar, M. C., Waters, E., & Wall, S. (1978). *Patterns of attachment: A psychological study of the strange situation.* Hillsdale, NJ: Erlbaum.

Alliance of Psychoanalytic Organizations. (2006). *Psychodynamic diagnostic manual.* Silver Springs, MD: Author.

American Psychiatric Association. (2000). *Diagnostic and statistical manual of mental disorders* (4th ed., text rev.). Arlington, VA: Author.

Baldwin, S. A., Wampold, B. E., & Imel, Z. E. (2007). Untangling the alliance-outcome correlation: Exploring the relative importance of therapist and patient variability in the alliance. *Journal of Consulting and Clinical Psychology, 75,* 842–852.

Balint, A., & Balint, M. (1939). On transference and countertransference. *International Journal of Psychoanalysis, 20,* 223–230.

Barber, J. (2000). Alliance predicts patients' outcome beyond in-treatment change in symptoms. *Journal of Consulting and Clinical Psychology, 68,* 1027–1032.

Beck, J. S. (1995). *Cognitive therapy.* New York: Guilford Press.

Bowlby, J. (1969). *Attachment.* New York: Basic Books.

Bowlby, J. (1973). *Separation.* Basic Books.

Bowlby, J. (1980). *Loss.* Basic Books.

Cozolino, L. (2002). *The neuroscience of psychotherapy.* New York: Norton.

Cozolino, L. (2006). *The neuroscience of human relationships.* New York: Norton.

Doweicko, H. E. (2002). *Concepts of chemical dependency,* Belmont, CA: Brooks/Cole.

Dozier, M., & Kobak, R. (1992). Psychophysiology in attachment interviews: Converging evidence for deactivating strategies. *Child Development, 63,* 1473–1480.

Dunbar, R. I. (1996). *Grooming, gossip, and the evolution of language.* Cambridge, MA: Harvard University Press.

Erikson, E. (1950). *Childhood and society.* New York: Norton.

Fliess, R. (1942). The metapsychology of the analyst. *Psychoanalytic Quarterly, 11,* 211–227.

Fosha, D., Siegal, D. J., & Solomon, M. F. (2009). *The healing power of emotion: Affective neuroscience, development and clinical practice.* New York: Norton.

Freud, S. (1912). *Recommendations to physicians practicing psychoanalysis* (standard ed.). London: Hogarth Press.

Freud, S. (1960). *The ego and the id* (Trans. James Strachey). New York: Norton.

Freud, S. (1966). *Introductory lectures on psychoanalysis* (Trans. James Strachey). New York: Norton.

Gallese, V. (2001). "The shared manifold" hypothesis: From mirror neurons to empathy. *Journal of Consciousness Studies, 8*(5–7), 33–50.

Gendlin, E. T. (1978). *Focusing.* New York: Everest House.

Gilligan, C. (1982). *In a different voice.* Cambridge, MA: Harvard University Press.

Giovacchini, P. (1981). Countertransference and therapeutic turmoil. *Contemporary Psychoanalysis, 17,* 565–594.

Greenspan, S. I., & Shanker, S. G. (2006). A developmental framework for depth psychology and a definition of healthy emotional functioning. In Alliance of Psychoanalytic Organizations, *The psychodynamic diagnostic manual* (n.p.). Silver Spring, MD: Author.

Grinberg, L. (1962). On a specific aspect of countertransference due to the patient's projective identification. *International Journal of Psychoanalysis,* 436–440.

Heimann, P. (1950). On countertransference. *International Journal of Psychoanalysis, 31,* 81–84.

Hepworth, D. H., Rooney, R. H., & Larsen, J. (2006). *Direct social work practice: Theory and skills* (7th ed.). Belmont, CA: Thomson–Brooks/Cole.

Hubble, M., Duncan, B., & Miller, S. (1999). *The heart and soul of change: What works in therapy.* Washington, DC: American Psychological Association.

Klauber, J. (1968). The psychoanalyst as a person. *British Journal of Medical Psychology, 33,* 315–322.

Klein, M. (1946). Notes on some schizoid mechanisms. *International Journal of Psychoanalysis, 27,* 99–110.

Kohut, H. (1971). *Analysis of the self.* New York: International Universities Press.

Lacan, J. (1968). *The language of the self: The function of language in psychoanalysis* (Trans. Anthony Wilden). Baltimore: Johns Hopkins University Press.

Lambert, M., & Barley, D. (2001). Research summary on the therapeutic relationship and psychotherapy outcome. *Psychotherapy, 38*(4), 357–361.

Leichsenring, F., & Rabung, S. (2008). Effectiveness of long-term psychodynamic psychotherapy: A meta-analysis. *Journal of the American Medical Association, 300*(13), 1551–1565.

Levin, J. D. (2001). *Therapeutic strategies for treating addiction.* New York: Aronson.

Little, M. I. (1981). *Transference neurosis and transference psychosis.* New York: Aronson.

Lyons-Ruth, K., & Boston Change Process Study Group. (2001). The emergence of new experiences: Relational improvisation, recognition process and non-linear change in psychoanalytic psychotherapy. *Psychologist/Psychoanalyst, 21*(4), 13–17.

Mahler, M. S., Pine, F., & Bergman, A. (1975). *The psychological birth of the human infant.* New York: Basic Books.

McKenzie, F. R. (1995). *A study of clinical social workers' recognition and use of countertransference with adult borderline clients* (Doctoral dissertation). Available from UMI Dissertation Services (UMI No. 9543475).

McKenzie, F. R. (1999, June). *The clinical validation method: Use of self in the therapeutic relationship.* Paper presented at the International Conference for the Advancement of Private Practice of Clinical Social Work, Charleston, SC.

McKenzie, F. R. (2008). *Theory and practice with adolescents: An applied approach.* Chicago: Lyceum Books.

Meeks, J. E., & Bernet, W. (2001). *The fragile alliance* (5th ed.). Malabar, FL: Krieger.

Minnix, J. A., Reitzel, L. R., & Pepper, K. A. (2005). Total number of MMPI-2 clinical scale elevations predicts premature termination after controlling for intake symptom severity and personality disorder diagnosis. *Personality and Individual Differences, 38*(8), 1745–1755.

Mitchell, S. A. (1988). *Relational concepts in psychoanalysis: An integration.* Cambridge, MA: Harvard University Press.

Morrow, D. F. (2004). Social work practice with gay, lesbian, bisexual, and transgender adolescents. *Families in Society, 85*(1), 91–99.

Ogden, T. (1982). *Projective identification and psychotherapeutic technique.* New York: Aronson

Palumbo, J. (1983). Spontaneous self disclosures in psychotherapy. *Clinical Social Work Journal, 15*, 691–704.

Powers, G. T., Meenaghan, T. M., & Toomey, B. G. (1985). *Practice focused research.* Upper Saddle River, NJ: Prentice-Hall.

Prochaska, J. O., & Norcross, J. C. (2003). *Systems of psychotherapy: A transtheoretical analysis* (5th ed.). Florence, KY: Thomson Brooks/Cole.

Racker, H. (1968). *Transference and countertransference.* London: Hogarth Press.

Rizzolatti, G., & Arbib, M.A. (1998). Language within our grasp. *Trends in Neuroscience, 21*(5), 188–194.

Rogers, C. R. (1957). The necessary and sufficient conditions of therapeutic personality change. *Journal of Consulting Psychology, 21,* 95–103.

Rogers, C. R. (1961). *On becoming a person.* Boston: Houghton-Mifflin.

Rogers, C. R. (1965). *Client-centered therapy.* Boston: Houghton-Mifflin.

Rothman, J. C. (2008). *Cultural competence in process and practice.* Boston: Allyn and Bacon/Pearson.

Saari, C. (1986). The created relationship: Transference and countertransference and the therapeutic culture. *Clinical Social Work Journal, 14,* 39–51.

Schachner, D. A., Shauer, P. R., & Mikulincer, M. (2005). Patterns of nonverbal behavior and sensitivity in attachment relations. *Journal of Nonverbal Behavior, 29*(3), 141–169.

Searles, H. F. (1979). *Countertransference.* New York: International Universities Press.

Shevrin, H. (2006). The contribution of cognitive behavioral and neurophysiological frames of reference to a psychodynamic nosology of mental illness. In Alliance of Psychoanalytic Organizations, *Psychodynamic diagnostic manual* (n.p.). Silver Spring, MD: Author.

Shulman, S. R. (2009). *The skills of helping individuals, families, groups and communities* (6th ed.). Belmont, CA: Brooks/Cole.

Siegel, D. J. (1999). *The developing brain.* New York: Guilford Press.

Stampley, C., & Slaght, E. (2004). Cultural competence as a clinical obstacle. *Smith College Studies in Social Work, 74*(2), 333–347.

Stern, D. N. (1985). *The interpersonal world of the human infant.* New York: Basic Books.

Tansey, M. J., & Burke, W. F. (1989). *Understanding countertransference: From projective identification to empathy.* Mahwah, NJ: Analytic Press.

Wallin, D. J. (2007). *Attachment in psychotherapy.* New York: Guilford Press.

Walsh, J. (2007). *Endings in clinical practice: Effective closure in diverse settings* (2nd ed.). Chicago: Lyceum Books.

Weaver, H. N. (2005). *Explorations in cultural competence.* Florence, KY: Thomson.

Winnicott, D. W. (1949). Hate in the countertransference. *International Journal of Psychoanalysis, 30,* 69–74.

Winnicott, D. W. (1953). Transitional objects and transitional phenomena: A study of the first not-me possession. *International Journal of Psychoanalysis, 34*, 89–97.

Winnicott, D. W. (1965). *The maturational processes and the facilitating environment.* New York: International Universities Press.

Winnicott, D. W. (1971). *Playing and reality.* New York: Routledge.

Zastrow, C. (1999). *The practice of social work* (6th ed.). Pacific Grove, CA: Brooks/Cole.

Selected Bibliography

Adler, A. (1963). *The practice and theory of individual psychology.* Totowa, NJ: Littlefield.

Bandura, A. (1977). *Social learning theory.* Upper Saddle River, NJ: Prentice Hall.

Beck, A. (1976). *Cognitive theory and the emotional disorders.* New York: International Universities Press.

Cozolino, L. (2004). *The making of a therapist: A practice guide for the inner journey.* New York: Norton.

De Shazer, S., & Berg, I. K. (1997). *Interviewing for solutions.* Pacific Grove, CA: Brooks/Cole.

Elias, L. J., & Saucier, D. M. (2006). *Neuropsychology.* Boston: Pearson.

Elson, M. (1986). *Self psychology in clinical social work.* New York: Norton.

Franklin, C., & Jordan, C. (2003). An integrative skills assessment approach. In C. Jordan & C. Franklin (Eds.), *Clinical assessment for social workers: Quantitative and qualitative methods* (2nd ed., pp. 1–52). Chicago: Lyceum Books.

Gendlin, E. T. (1969). Focusing. *Psychotherapy: Theory, Research and Practice, 6,* 14–15.

Goldstein, E. (1995). *Ego psychology and social work practice.* New York: Free Press.

Greenspan, S. I., & Shanker, S. G. (2006). A developmental framework for depth psychology and a definition of healthy emotional functioning. In Alliance of Psychoanalytic Organizations, *The psychodynamic diagnostic manual* (n.p.). Silver Springs, MD: Author.

Gurman, A. S. (1977). The patient's perception of the therapeutic relationship. In A. S. Gurman & A. M. Razin (Eds.), *Effective psychotherapy: A handbook of research* (pp. 503–543). New York: Oxford University Press.

Gurman, A. S., & Razin, A. M. (1977). *Effective psychotherapy: A handbook of research.* New York: Oxford University Press.

Jaynes, J. (1976). *The origins of consciousness in the breakdown of the bicameral mind.* Boston: Houghton Mifflin.

Johnson, S. M., & Whiffen, V. E. (2003). *Attachment processes in couple and family therapy.* New York: Guilford Press.

Luborsky, L., Crits-Christoph, P., Mintz, J., & Auerbach, A. (1988). *Who will benefit from psychotherapy?* New York: Basic Books.

Monk, G., Winslade, J., Crocket, K., & Epston, D. (1997). *Narrative therapy in practice.* San Francisco: Jossey-Bass.

Morrow, D. (1993). Social work with gay and lesbian adolescents. *Social Work, 38*(6), 655–660.

Morrow, D. F. (2004). Social work practice with gay, lesbian, bisexual, and transgender adolescents. *Families in Society, 85*(1), 91–99.

Nichols, M. P., & Schwartz, R. C. (2006). *Family therapy: Concepts and methods* (7th ed.). New York: Pearson, Allyn and Bacon.

O'Hare, T. (2005). *Evidence-based practices for social workers.* Chicago: Lyceum Books.

Pausch, R. (2008). *The last lecture.* New York: Hyperion.

Pavlov, I. P. (1927). *Conditioned reflexes.* London: Oxford University Press.

Perls, F. (1969). *Gestalt therapy verbatim.* Moab, UT: Real Person Press.

Perls, F. (1973). *The gestalt approach.* Palo Alto, CA: Science and Behavior Books.

Pinel, J. (2006). *Biopsychology.* Boston: Pearson.

Roseborough, D. G. (2006). Psychodynamic psychotherapy: An effectiveness study. *Research on Social Work Practice, 16,* 166–175.

Roth, A., & Fonagy, P. (1996). *What works for whom? A critical review of psychotherapy research.* New York: Guilford Press.

Russell, R. L. (Ed.). (1994). *Reassessing psychotherapy research.* New York: Guilford Press.

Saleebey, D. (Ed.). (1997). *The strengths perspective in social work practice.* Boston: Allyn and Bacon.

Santrock, J. W. (2006). *Life-span development* (10th ed.). New York: McGraw-Hill.

Shulman, S. R. (1999). *Termination of short-term and long-term psychotherapy: Patients' and therapists' affective reactions and therapists' technical management (attachment style, therapy model).* Dissertation Abstracts International, 60, 6B.

Skinner, B. F. (1953). *Science and human behavior.* New York: Macmillan.

Stampley, C., & Slaght, E. (2004). Cultural competence as a clinical obstacle. *Smith College Studies in Social Work, 74*(2), 333–347.

Sullivan, H. S. (1953). *The interpersonal theory of psychiatry.* New York: Norton.

Index

CPSIA information can be obtained
at www.ICGtesting.com
Printed in the USA
BVHW062131241121
622491BV00008B/172